Focus on the Love

A Transformative Approach to Organizational Leadership

Akbar Cook

OSG PUBLICATIONS
NEW YORK, NEW YORK

FOCUS ON THE LOVE

DEDICATION

This book is dedicated to my maternal grandmother, Almeta Cook. My very first memories about unconditional love start with her.

As toddlers, when Grandma came home from work, we had to sing along with her. "Save some sugar (kisses) for Grandma. That's what Mommy says." So one day, I didn't even let her put down her bags and ran to her. "Grandma, Grandma, I got some sugar for you!" The mother of six children, she still had room in her heart to be a foster parent to countless disadvantaged youth. The love didn't stop there because Grandma was instrumental in getting five of them adopted into the Cook household. To this very day, if you put all of her grandchildren and great grandchildren in a room, you wouldn't know who was adopted and who wasn't. They are my family; they are my cousins regardless of the blood line. That's the true testament of unconditional love.

I don't know if it's cultural, but we grew up in a household where if one child got in trouble, then everyone got in trouble. It usually went like this: Nikki and Karriem were in trouble because they were the oldest and should've known better. Poor Rahman and I tried to tiptoe by and got in trouble as well for not taking the garbage out three days ago. At that time, I thought it was wrong because I usually was one of the good grandkids (LOL). However, this is a tool that most parents use to show there's no favoritism at play among the children. There was never a shortage of grandchildren at Grandma's house with at least four of us living with her every day for over 30 years. This unconditional love didn't stop there. Many of our childhood friends became her grandchildren as well. I can recall my best friend/cousin, Marc Taylor, staying the weekend at Grandma's and I wasn't even there. Or the time my college friends, Eric and J.T., couldn't afford to stay longer, so Grandma paid for their tickets to stay an additional two weeks. The funny thing was, I was working so they stayed at the house with Grandma all day kicking it. It's safe to say that they're all family now. The Cook "Home Sweet Home" had a foundation built on love.

At the time I'm writing this, we're two weeks away from my Grandma's 92nd birthday. Grandma has outlived all of her siblings, and her childhood friends. More importantly, she's buried three of her children. I can't even imagine the strength it takes to carry on, but I do know what keeps her going: the love for the ones that are still living. Not a second goes by where the love for my family doesn't will me to do things to make my ancestors proud. The last two years have been nothing short of amazing, but knowing my mom and Grandma are here to enjoy it with me means the world to me. Grandma has instilled love in our DNA. Just as all of us were Grandma's "babies," whom she loved and cherished, so I too love my "babies," the students who I serve.

"Grandma, Grandma, I really got some sugar for you!"

In loving memory of Almeta Cook

October 28, 1928 -November 10, 2020

CONTENTS

AN INTRODUCTION

If you look around today, you will see various examples of leadership. From an elected local official to a school principal, leadership is a position that we, as a society, often hold in high regards. While there are many people in positions of leadership today, there are only a few who display the true qualities of a leader. More often than not, we come across many leaders who are authoritative, unapproachable, figureheads, dictators or people who lead with passive-aggressive styles. Some even occupy leadership positions because of the benefits they can derive, so by the time their tenure has expired, they leave those whom they led worse than they were before, often, bankrupt, dry and bereft of any good skills or growth.

Yes, it is true that there are different types of and levels of leadership. Some might seem more important and more favorable than others. But the fact is that no matter the position one has as a leader, he/she is still a leader. Furthermore, leadership isn't exclusively about the number of people one leads. Ranging from the President of the United States, the managing director of a big company, the director of a healthcare facility, the owner of beauty salon to the head custodian in a school, the pastor of a church, a parent, the principal of a school, or the teacher in a classroom, these are all examples of leaders. Additionally, all of the people listed above share the fact that they hold important positions and have the power to influence the people whom they lead. They have employees and people who look up to them, people with whom they have to work together to achieve certain goals and meet objectives to make the vision of an organization a reality. Therefore, as a leader or an aspiring leader, it is vital to make a good impression on your team members so that you won't be termed as a person who is "off limits." It is also important to keep in mind that you have a team to work with, a team to develop/coach, and a team with whom you want to achieve optimal results. As such, the big question becomes: "How will you, as a leader, achieve these goals with your team in the best possible way?"

The answer, I contend, is with *love,* the four-letter word that is so often heard and over used, and even sadly neglected by many who occupy positions of leadership. Yes, the key is love. Leading without love leads to a 99.9% likelihood of failure. Conversely, leadership founded on genuine love creates the most magnificent results. If we think about many of the great leaders in history and even in the influential leaders in our own lives, we will probably recognize that great stories of leadership have their foundations anchored in love. The love talked about here is not the warm, fuzzy feeling of romantic love that sends one blushing and conjuring up sweet texts for the other party. No. Although there is great value in that type of love, it is not the definition of love that is drawn from throughout this book.

The love here is a propelling force; it is the fuel that drives one to push further to make the best of their position; it is the fuel with which we chase our passions; it is the fuel with which we energize; and it is the fuel with which we find happiness, peace, and pleasure. It's that energy derived from loving what we do and how we do it and then spreading that love to our colleagues to grow an organization or meet/exceed its vision or mission. A true leader leaves a legacy. A leader wants to keep others talking positively about their time together, no matter how long the duration. Most importantly, leaders set examples and create other leaders who will keep on imparting the world and improving their spheres of influence.

For this reason, it is important to note that the love discussed throughout *Focus on the Love* can be interchanged with the words "passion" or "devotion." This love comes from the heart, that organ which drives human emotion, and as long as the heart is there, the love should never die. Leading with love is an effective and proven approach to all variations of leadership which can enhance employee interaction, employee well-being, and employee production—all of which lead to a better society in which we interact and live in. Even if you don't have employees, you may still have team members or mentees. Regardless of the context the key to effective leadership is the ability to build healthy relationships grounded in love with those whom we lead.

In order to contextualize this, I draw from the pivotal text, *The Spark, The Flame, and the Torch: Inspire Self, Inspire Others, Inspire the World.* written by leadership guru Lance Secretan (2010). He states that:

> The degree to which each of us is inspiring is determined by the degree to which each of us is inspired ourselves. Uninspired people cannot inspire other people—it isn't within them. In fact, no one can inspire another person unless they themselves are inspired—parent, CEO, minister, firefighter, politician, rock star, author—no one. We experience the world not as it is, but

as we are. Inspired people, therefore, cannot help themselves from inspiring others—it radiates from within them and affects everyone around them, because that is who they are. (pp. 3-4)

Here, Secretan reminds us that leading is not about techniques or methods; rather, it is about inspiring others from the heart. This model of leadership can be deemed as one that allows love to move you into making the decision to be fully attentive to the position you occupy, as well being inspirational to your team in order to achieve the best results. It suggests that no matter what the procedures and approaches are that you adopt in leading, if any of them are done without the basis of love, involvement, and consideration of others, they are nothing.

Most religious texts provide guidance for our interactions with others. For example, both the Torah and the Christian Bible espouse us to, "Love thy neighbor as thyself"(Matthew 22:39 and Leviticus 19:18). This foundational belief is also echoed in Islam, Hindu and Buddhism. Regardless of one's belief system, the concept of being a part of a community anchored in love is a constant reminder that with a focus on love and respect for one's team members, you display emotional intelligence and provide a safe space for the growth of other's professional skill sets and personal, emotional intelligence.

Understandably, this leads to the question of: How does one lead with love? I hope that with the strategies and stories that I explore throughout this book, you will find methods and techniques that can be implemented in your leadership style. As such, *Focus on the Love* aims to help sincere leaders discover how leading with love can be made possible and how great things can be achieved by the great power of love. It's a different strategy than many of us learned in school and/or on the job; yet, when implemented with fidelity, it will lead to positive outcomes.

Anyone can occupy a leadership position, but what differentiates a true leader from just a position "holder" is the ability of the former to lead with a focus on love. For example, consider parenting methods: The ideal parent showers their children with love in hopes of their children achieving more success than themselves. In other words, many of us adapt as we see fit. On occasion, "tough love" needs to be exercised. This strong emotional connection can also be implemented in your professional work environment. Focusing on love is powerful. As Glenn C. Steward (2016) indicated: "If leadership is truly grounded in love, you'll always land in the category of a good leader" ("Developing Super Leaders," para.1).

Chapter 1

THE CONCEPT OF LEADERSHIP

"A leader takes people where they want to go. A great leader takes people where they don't necessarily want to go but ought to be."
-Rosalynn Carter

Being a leader involves a great number of responsibilities; it is not just occupying a leadership position. Yes, it is true that there are quite a number of people who are called leaders, whether at the religious, social, economic, and/or political levels, but not all of them display the qualities and virtues of a leader. Anyone can be termed a leader, but true and effective leaders are known by the actions that they perform, the lives and situations they transform, and the great legacies they leave behind. In other words, a great leader is not known by the position they occupy, but by the actions they perform.

For many of us, the term leader is used so loosely that we don't stop to think about its actual meaning and its implications. Here, I'd like to offer a few views that give us insight about the answer to: Who then is a Leader?

"Good leaders must first become good servants."
Robert Greenleaf

"A leader is one who knows the way, goes the way, and shows the way."
Warren G. Bennis

"Before you are a leader, success is all about growing yourself. When you become a leader, success is all about growing others."
Jack Welch

"Leadership is practiced not so much in words as in attitude and in actions."
Harold S. Geneen

As you reflect upon each of these quotes, it becomes clear that each definition emphasizes a particular component of leadership. The last definition, in particular, suggests that leadership is viewed as displaying certain actions rather than engaging in just empty words and promises. The first and second definitions view good leaders as those who build others up and make the best out of them. They are also those who transform the lives of others and create leaders out of them. In essence, a good leader must be a guide to other people by showing the way, helping others and developing others.

Collectively, these definitions agree that a good leader is a teacher, guide, person of understanding, builder, person of great attitude and actions (not just words of mouth), performer, plus a starter and finisher. All of these are actions that require hard work to bring out extraordinary results in others. When Vince Lombardi (2020) stated that, "Leaders aren't born, they are made. And they are made just like anything else, through hard work. And that's the price we'll have to pay to achieve that goal, or any goal," he understood that leadership requires a work ethic (as cited in Newell, para.1). There are numerous people in positions of leadership, but what differentiates a true leader from others who are not is the ability to serve as a catalyst for great changes through one's actions.

With a working understanding of what is required to become a leader, one understands that it requires hard work. In other words, there are certain qualities that a leader must possess in order to be impactful and to maximize growth. The following list is not exhaustive; yet, it includes many of the attributes that captains of industry, world leaders, and educational leaders alike share in common.

Characteristics and Attributes of Exceptional Leaders

Vision

A vision is the starting point of seeing something become an actual reality. You have to be able to see something even before it manifests. A good leader can see what he/she wants to accomplish even before he/she begins the quest. As such, the concept of vision does not have to do with the physical sense of sight. Rather, it refers to a leader's ability to have a particular goal that he/she is working towards. Some may think of this skill as having foresight or the ability to foresee or prepare wisely for the future. A leader must have a goal that he/she wants to accomplish with a set of people who are on the same team with him/her. This suggests that one major factor that qualifies one for the position of leadership is the vision factor. A leader must be able to ask and answer the questions: Where are we going to?, What do we want to achieve?, and How are we going to get here? Vision can be likened to driving towards a particular destination. It would be outright absurd if one decides to hop in a vehicle and start driving without a clear sense of one's destination. Even before starting the vehicle, one must know where their destination is and the route one must take in order to get to that destination. The same is analogous to being a leader—it all starts with a vision about one's goals, outcomes, and ultimate destination.

When Theodore Hesburgh (2015) stated: "The very essence of leadership is that you have to have a vision," he emphasized the words 'have to' which suggests that vision is a very compulsory quality that a leader must have in order to be qualified for the leadership position (as cited in Dees, para. 1). You have to know where you are headed before you answer to the name "leader." After this has been established then you can share your vision with your team and, together, work collaboratively towards reaching a particular destination.

If a vision hasn't been established, then you can be likened to a group of people operating blindly and there is a strong probability that you will not have optimal results. Perhaps James Kouzes and Barry Posner (2017) state it best when they conceded that, "And we've also found that in the best organizations, everyone, regardless of title or position, is encouraged to act like a leader. That's because in these places, people don't just believe that everyone can make a difference; they act in ways to develop and grow people's talents, including their leadership capabilities"(p. 14).

While it is compulsory as a leader to have a vision mindset, it is also necessary that one is optimistic about the vision. Having a negative mindset towards the goal you want to achieve will serve as an impediment or a hurdle. You must have confidence that the goal is obtainable. As a leader, the people around you will be able to sense if you truly believe that a goal is realistic. Everything from the language you use, the people you select on the team, and the directives you give should clearly reflect confidence in your vision.

Again, as a leader, having the *knowledge* of the type of goal you want to achieve is also very important. Warren G. Bennis (2009) captures why this is important when he states, "Vision, inspiration, empathy, trustworthiness are manifestations of a leader's judgment and character"(p. 133). In order to know the way, a leader must have a vision which lays out clear steps to attain that vision, including having a general and intricate understanding of what the goal is about. This is interconnected with the idea of having an *understanding*. Yes, knowledge is important; however, understanding involves reasoning and displaying your intelligence as well as using acquired and inferred knowledge in its proper context. Finally, wisdom is also a tool that helps a leader fulfil the vision; it is the ability to use one's intuition in making certain goal-driven decisions. Wisdom is the ability to make decisions based on the combination of your knowledge, experience and understanding. Furthermore, it is knowing right from wrong decisions and actions in certain contexts.

Courage

The Greek Philosopher Aristotle (2014) once stated, "Take the case of justice and courage; if everybody were just, there would be no use for courage, whereas all might be courageous, and still justice would be of use"(as cited in Ross, p. 384). Undoubtedly, it is expected that one will face challenging situations in the course of driving towards a specific goal. It is how one operates as a leader during these challenging situations that will determine the level of one's courage. You must know that the vision you are aiming for will have its good and bad sides and, as a leader, you must be ready to bear the brunt of the bad sides and show others how something ought to be done.

Think about the movie *Speed* with Keanu Reeves and Sandra Bullock. Imagine if the driver of a bus decides to jump out when the brakes fail, and there are quite a number of people still on the bus. If he jumps out, we can only imagine that the bus will definitely keep on running and eventually crash, causing fatalities. In this scenario, the driver of this bus has not displayed courage in any way nor has he displayed leadership. Instead, he buckled out when his team needed him the most and this had a drastic effect. He set out with his team, agreeing to take them towards a particular destination without considering that leadership, at times, requires sacrifice.

As foolish as it may sound, what a courageous person ought to do in a situation like this is try, as much as possible within his/her power, to get the bus to safety and assure the team that safety is a priority. This may be done by finding an obstacle like a tree to stop the bus or quickly finding an alternate route with the least amount of traffic to minimize further damage. This example helps us understand that a leader must be able to face challenges and consequences in the process of driving towards the vision. In doing so, he/she must also assure the team that they would get out of an unfortunate or distressful situation in a timely manner. This is where the idea of sacrifice comes in. In the above scenario, the bus driver must decide if he will lead by example with the expectation that the others will follow. Further reminding us of John Kenneth Galbraith's (2017) claim that, "All of the great leaders have had one characteristic in common; it was the willingness to confront unequivocally the major anxiety of their people in their time. This, and not much else, is the essence of leadership"(as cited in *Smart Brief*, para. 1). As a leader, it is my hope that you will never find yourself in a life/death situation; however, acts of courage do not have to be that extreme. Courage is a powerful tool in breaking records and carrying your team along. It is also, according to Aristotle, a noble act. Once the courage is there, a leader will be able to accomplish almost anything.

Integrity

Integrity is derived from one's ability to be honest. Additionally, we often attach integrity to one's morals and values. A leader who lacks integrity is a highly problematic leader and I wonder if such a person is really a leader. Because of this, integrity in leadership cannot be overemphasized. In fact, Dwight D. Eisenhower (2013), the 34th President of the United States remarked:

> In order to be a leader a man must have followers. And to have followers, a man must have their confidence. Hence, the supreme quality of a leader is unquestionably integrity. Without it, no real success is possible, no matter whether it is on a section gang, on a football field, in an army, or in an office. If a man's associates find him guilty of phoniness, if they find that he lacks forthright integrity, he will fail. His teachings and actions must square with each other (as cited in Kisel, para. 1).

As Eisenhower reminds us, you cannot afford to have a bad name or character. Your reputation cannot be tarnished. If you do, your team will begin to question your efficacy. With integrity comes transparency and accountability.

A transparent person is an honest person and honesty is one of the characteristics of integrity. Transparency involves being open, not hiding secrets from one's team members, not even in the name of protecting them from the hard truth. Whether hard or soft, the truth remains the truth and it deserves to be known to avoid the spread of misinformation. If we expect this of others, we must reflect this in our actions and deeds.

As a leader, you should take note that you are not leading yourself but you are leading others, and it is paramount that you work together as a team to accomplish your goal. This is best done when everyone is open, honest, and truthful. As the leader you must be transparent with your team. They deserve to know what the issues are and how to best protect the organization.

In leading with transparency, you build trust with your team. Together you work collaboratively to remove the barriers. Imagine being on the other end and having your key personnel withholding vital information from you. No matter how hard or grievous the truth is, it deserves to be known by your group members because you all are in it together. It takes a great deal of courage to decide to tell the truth no matter how hard it may be. To avoid any form of mistrust or questions about your honesty, the best thing is to be transparent at all times. Aristotle (2014) says that, "For though we love both [the truth and our friends], piety requires us to honor the truth first"(as cited in Ross, p. 6). We must honor the truth at all times to avoid drastic consequences of being shady or dishonest.

Similarly, while transparency involves being honest, accountability has to do with being responsible for your actions. Yes, leaders sometimes make mistakes or some wrong decisions because they are humans, and no human is definitely perfect. Therefore, being courageous means being accountable, regardless of the consequences. If you know you are wrong, accept it. Own up to your errors. A great leader recognizes that being honest is an act that a leader must display and instill in his/her followers. When you do something wrong or below expectations, you must be held accountable for it and never try to rope an innocent person in because that is an act of cowardice. Cowardice is kryptonite for transformational leadership. Leadership requires courage which builds trust and shows the team that you are not perfect which makes you a stronger leader. All we have in this world is our word. If that means nothing to you, neither does your leadership.

Humility

Humility has to do with thinking low of one's self, claiming little for one's self, and not being too proud or arrogant. Great leaders need to learn a great degree of humility, as it will help them to a large extent. Humility makes you not think of yourself more than you ought to. One may be tempted as a leader in his/her position to feel proud and arrogant, but a true leader will know that pride only makes the situation worse. Furthermore, team members may not be encouraged to relate with an unrelatable leader. This will not end well as a leader needs his/her followers in every way to be able to attain the goal that everyone is aspiring towards.

In fact, being a leader requires you to serve first before leading. Robert Greenleaf (2015) suggests that a leader's strength is grounded in his/her ability to also serve. Leaders, in turn, must think of others first before thinking of themselves; they must have the best interest of the team members at heart. This includes being polite and respectful to *all* team members. Once these gestures are displayed, they will be reciprocated. With humility comes selflessness or the willingness to consider others first, not just oneself. No leader has all of the knowledge in the world; it would be a fallacy to think in such a way. For this reason, a leader who humbles him/herself to the process of learning, growing, and evolving can learn from his/her teammates. Some team members might have extensive experience in an area or others may have institutional knowledge. A humble leader will want to learn from others to make his/her tenure productive and successful. Therefore, asking for help or assistance is a reflection of a leader's strength, not weakness.

Regardless of your credentials, education, or years of experience, lead with humility. It makes you all the more relatable and real, especially when compared to a leader who acts as if he/she knows everything. Such team members will get fed up listening to the leader brag about his/her accomplishments and accolades. Bit by bit, the leader begins to lose his/her credibility and, eventually, the team will be disinterested. As a leader, or an aspiring leader, be humble when relating with others, be selfless, be ready to learn, even if you have an idea already (no knowledge is lost), and be willing to serve, instead of being in the position for selfish reasons. Also, remember the three magic phrases that many of us learned during our childhood: "Thank you;" "I am sorry;" and "Please." These pleasantries should not be difficult for a leader to use in appreciating, apologizing and beseeching their team members.

Unlike humility, excessive pride can be highly problematic for any leader. Being humble and being ready to show your team that you are not perfect does not make you any less of a leader. It doesn't make you ineffective or weak. Conversely, it shows that you are original and willing to develop not only yourself but your team members as well. Humility allows you to lead by example and once your team members see you are not being a fake version of yourself, they will gain more confidence in you and will not hesitate to work with you.

Strategic Planning

Strategic planning and thinking are a process in which the leader plans and maps out how the organization will meet the agreed upon vision. The best leaders have the foresight to plan and organize stages of development while delegating human capital based on appropriate skill sets to meet the specific goals aligned to the vision.

Planning effectively requires formulating ideas and embarking on actions that are intended to accomplish a specific goal, including setting milestones to reflect and check in on those goals. The more you are able to plan, the more you will move the team towards the vision. Remember, inspect what you expect! If you don't hold team members accountable with helping to achieve the goal and with assisting with implanting the strategic plan, some may start to slack or become disengaged.

To offset this, stay innovative. Innovation is vital in the strategic planning process. With innovation comes creativity, which is the quality or ability to create or invent something. Once you are able to think of an innovative way to carry out the process of reaching your goal, then creativity comes in. Both work hand-in-hand. The journey towards achieving the goal will be easier and have a much more powerful effect on the outcome. Also be sure to tap into the creativity of your team members.

When drafting and thinking about your strategic plan, the leader and leadership team need to be innovative with solutions. It is easy to recognize the problems so make sure that you are solution-centric. Innovation is using your creative juices, thinking out of the box, and finding different remedies to an existing problem to remove the explicit and implied barriers. From Milton Hershey and Reginald Lewis to Bill Gates and Oprah Winfrey, all leaders must embrace innovation. A leader has to be ahead in his/her thinking in order for others to say: "I wish I could have thought of that first." When a team knows that their leader is a person of innovation, they will feel motivated to continue in the pursuit of the goal. An innovative leader sparks intrinsic motivation in their employees and this is reflected in how the team members respond. This intrinsic motivation empowers the employees with troubleshooting skills and critical thinking skills aligned to the strategic plan.

Team Work

As a school leader, empowering others is something that I must embrace. I realize that my team—comprised of assistant principals, department chairs, teachers, our administrative staff, and facilities workers—are all paying attention to how I lead. Over the course of the past four years, I have taken a hip-hop slang term and applied it to my own team building philosophy: "Match my fly."

In colloquial terms, this phrase normally means to use my fashion sense to style your own closet. Professionally, I use this concept to remind my team that they will need to match my work ethic, passion, love for what we do, humbleness, transparency, innovation, integrity, and efforts to build positive relationships with *all* stakeholders. In order to work with me, you need to, "Match my fly." It sets the tone for high expectations and layers of accountability. If a team member is unwilling to grow and develop this train of thought, unfortunately, he/she won't be an effective team member. An ineffective team member hurts the entire team and eventually, must be removed. Therefore, it is important for all leaders to develop your team to match your own fly! When all team members are aligned to "match your fly," there is consistency in messaging and expectations.

No great leader can lead in isolation. If you think about just yourself, you will not have anyone to lead. Just as a coach needs players, a leader needs followers. A team can be defined as a group of people involved in the same activity and/or a group of people driving towards a particular goal. The leader builds and coaches his/her team. You will have people on your team who have strong skill sets, but they may lack empathy. You will have people who have weak skill sets, yet great drive and a willingness to learn. The goal is to display true caring and love for all of your team members to ensure you function cohesively. A leader is no island of knowledge and he/she must understand that he/she is the head of a team of people who have experiences, ideas, knowledge, creativity, and drive. All must work together to achieve the goal and that requires cooperation.

Cooperation has to do with receiving active help from a person or, in this case, a group of people. Each person on the team has their part to play in ensuring that the vision is articulated. So, a leader must ensure that each member of the team is actively involved and aware of the steps for accomplishing the goal, no matter how small. For this to be achieved, a leader must show compassion, empathy, and actualize Shakespeare's (1992) proverbial phrase from "Julius Caesar," *lend me your ears* (p. 121). A leader needs to make time to have a listening ear for the people on the team and a willingness to show compassion.

Compassion is showing that you care, not just through your words, but in your actions as well. There is an old, unattributed, adage that many of us are probably familiar with: "Actions speak louder than words." It is possible that when you ask one of your team members a question about how they feel about a particular thing or idea, they may want to give a mechanical answer because they may fear your response. They may also lack self-esteem in their own abilities and may not want to create a contentious relationship. But you, as a leader, have to show that you really care about their opinion. Through your interactions, body language, and responses, you have to show them that you are all in this together, and that their input is valued. This establishes a healthy bond that lets your team members know that you are asking for an honest response which should make them comfortable in sharing their opinions and ideas with you. This is where a listening ear comes in.

If, as a leader, you only speak with your words and not your actions or you don't listen attentively, your members will not feel comfortable sharing their innovative and creative ideas with you or the team. To counter this, welcome conversations with the people in your charge. Take notes and jot down their ideas and feedback to use for future reference. Nodding and making eye contact, while actually listening, will encourage them as well. Be sure to demonstrate patience and compassion in other areas too like family, personal matters, and professional interests.

When people know their leader generally cares, it will boost their confidence in meeting and talking with you. Focus on the end goals and outcomes and remember that goals are more easily accomplished collaboratively: "Focusing on contribution turns one of the inherent weaknesses of the executive's [or leader's] situation—his dependence on other people, his being within the organization—into a source of strength. It creates a team," says Peter Drucker (2006, p. 73). A great leader understands that their job is to make the team optimal in its function and productivity. They accept responsibility and don't sidestep it, recognizing that *we*, the team, will get the credit. This is what creates trust, and what enables a leader to get the task done. Therefore, a leader must ensure that all team members feel respected and appreciated, both personally and professionally, to function cohesively as a team.

Passion

Have you ever done something that you truly enjoyed? More than likely your desire to succeed at that something was derived from your passion. Passion is often a misused term; yet, it is critically important for leadership. Passion can also be synonymous with love, which is the most important quality that distinguishes a great leader from just any ordinary leader. Without love for what you do, the other qualities can become robotic and lack emotion. Love for the position you are in as a leader has to be established. As previously discussed in the book, love is the driving force that pushes you to embark on the journey towards that desired goal that you envision. Passion can fill in the gap when time and stamina become challenges. As Steve Jobs (2018) reminds all of us: "You have to have a lot of passion for what you are doing because it is so hard…if you do not, any rational person will give up" (as cited in Gallo, para. 3). As such, passion pushes you to break the boundaries, to go beyond the ordinary level for something you desire deeply and that is important to your team, group, community, organization, business, or school.

Leaders must be passionate about their positions in the sense that they transform it for the better. When you are passionate, you create better teammates in the course of aspiring them towards accomplishing a goal. This is quite a lot of hard work and serious dedication to the position of leadership; yet, it is doable with passion. At first, it may take practice to build the skill set for yourself and for all your team members.

For something that you love, you will want to ensure that you learn all that you can about it, to have vast knowledge about something and persevere by not giving up irrespective of what may arise. Being passionate about something means sacrificing, facing difficult situations and challenges, and most importantly seeing that you do not give up.

Quitting is not an option. Quitting is not a quality of leadership.

David Sarnoff, who founded NBC in 1926, once stated that we must love what we do in order to be successful at doing it (1986). That love, in turn, will serve as a compass. When you love something, you are willing to push through, even during difficult times. Loving what you do makes you bring out the best results from it, and also inspire others to do the same.

While many people may be in positions of leadership, some get there unprepared, and others are not aware of the demands or the responsibilities that the position entails. When focusing on the love, one must see oneself as responsible for those on one's team and together, everyone must work towards achieving the goals. This is the starting point of being a great leader. Love is the basis upon which all other qualities are founded. Genuine love provides a springboard to transform you as a leader. During the course of your leadership journey, you will learn and develop yourself, your team, and the position you are in, for the greater good. This is where focusing on the love makes a profound and measurable difference.

Chapter 2

WHAT KIND OF LEADER ARE YOU?

"Know Thyself."

The principle of "know thyself" has been attributed to ancient Greek philosophers. At the crux of this saying is the fundamental assumption that knowledge of self guides everything that we do. This is particularly true in leadership, regardless of one's industry or field. Imagine someone who is a basketball coach trying to motivate and encourage his/her players when the coach is not vested or interested in their success of growth. This lack of self-knowledge will impact how well the coach can truly connect with his players. Any leader who self-reflects and is aware of his/her style, strengths, and, yes, weaknesses has the potential to be a great leader.

Therefore, just as it is important to understand the qualities of a leader, it is of the essence to mention and discuss the various kinds of leaders that exist. Understanding each category and how it may impact your own leadership style will prevent you from being blindsided. It will also help you acknowledge both your strengths as well as areas that you may need to focus on to improve. The kinds of leaders discussed in this chapter are not exhaustive nor are they mutually exclusive. You may find that your style falls into one or more categories; therefore, think about how these styles can be applied to your leadership role in both global and specific ways.

Whether one is in education, business, entertainment, law, or corporate America, many of us have probably encountered a range of leaders. The types that I will explore below are intended to serve as a reference point as we venture into answering the question: What kind of leader are you?

The Managerial Leader

A managerial leader is one who occupies his/her position for the benefit of what he/she can derive from it. These kinds of leaders manage their positions by directing and controlling their team members. In fact, they are of the opinion that those whom they are leading are merely tools to be used in achieving self-made goals. They are mostly autocratic, self-centered and not people-centered. They make decisions by themselves and enforce them on others without asking for their opinions and input. The people under them merely follow just because they have to, not because they want to, and they have no relationship whatsoever with their leader. In cases like this, teamwork is often relegated to the background.

Leaders of this sort love to be served, rather than serving people. The love they display is not for their team members but for the fact that they occupy a position and that position will give them the benefits they desire. They are weak at developing others and building them up, and certainly, they are the least effective of the five types of leaders that have been identified.

These kinds of leaders leave without making any real growth in terms of character development or enhancing their team members, hence they are least impactful. It doesn't matter what amount of knowledge they have, as long as they do not use it for the greater good of others and in developing themselves, they will not make any influence. So, these leaders are weak in character and influence.

The Relational Leader

As the name implies, this type of leader is great with relating to people. Unlike the managerial leader, they love serving others and place people higher than the position in which they serve. Their ability to build relationships with others makes them liked by their teammates and this makes it easy for the relational leader to influence his/her teammates. Though their passion is to influence their teammates, a relational leader more often than not neglects the fact that he/she also needs to develop personally in order to become better at what they do. They just focus on the people they desire to influence and neither go further in carrying out necessary responsibilities in expanding their own knowledge about their positions nor focus on the further development of their character. At the end of the day, people only follow them because they are a people's person, not because they are knowledgeable about their positions.

So, while a relational leader is good at building relationships, he/she is weak at carrying out their necessary responsibilities of sacrificing and knowing more about their own leadership position. They derive their strengths from relationships with people but their weakness remains not carrying out the necessary responsibilities required of them as a leader. They are stronger in character than the managerial leader and good at influencing people.

The Motivational Leader

This kind of leader is driven towards influencing the team members and the organization they run. Like the relational leader, they are great at building relationships with people; they love serving people more than their positions which also makes it easy for them to influence people. But the motivational leader goes a step further in that they make an extra effort in seeking knowledge about their position of leadership so that people end up following them for the kind of person they are and for the knowledge they have. The motivational leader ends up influencing people outside of their team as well. A major weakness of the motivational leader is that he/she does not make special efforts in remaking more motivational leaders. They are theoretical in teaching and not practical. They influence others to a great extent, but they do not produce more motivational leaders.

A motivational leader is strong in influencing others, serving others, building relationships, getting results, knowledge, processes, and planning.

The Inspirational Leader

An inspirational leader is good at creating and helping develop other leaders. They inspire the managerial and relational leaders to grow to become motivational leaders. They are practical and people-based and love to serve. The inspirational leader has a major focus on character development. They grow and develop themselves in order to inspire others to grow as well. This is an instance of leading by example. They feel fulfilled when they begin to see others grow and develop into motivational leaders. These leaders are followed because of how much they care about other people and because of their characters. They produce great results and are good at helping others grow and evolve as leaders.

The Transformational Leader

A transformational leader is the strongest and most influential type of leader. They love to serve people; they value people more than their position and they make extra efforts into developing themselves, including their own character and the character of others. The content of their character is a key element. They are very passionate about transforming others and are highly respected because of this. They transform others into leaders too and their influence is so great that it spans across people, industries, organizations, several generations. They are the role models who other leaders look up to. Their influence continues to spread across generations. They leave a legacy behind that drives their followers into becoming transformational leaders too. They are highly developed in knowledge, have great planning strategies, know the value of teamwork, and are compassionate about their team members. Based on this definition, examples of transformational leaders across history are: Aristotle, Socrates, Gandhi, Alexander the Great, Queen Elizabeth I of England, Susan B. Anthony, Harriet Tubman, Abraham Lincoln, Martin Luther King Jr., Rosa Parks, Nelson Mandela, Steve Jobs, and Bill Gates.

Most transformational leaders often end up creating followers who also become greater and more influential than they are. They are driven by nothing other than passion, the love for their people, organization, and character development. This is aligned with Walter Lippman's (2019) view that "the final test of a leader is that he leaves behind him other men [and women] the conviction and the will to carry on"(as cited in Tulgan, para. 1). Furthermore, a person's character goes a long way in determining what sort of leader they will end up becoming. As leaders, no matter what, we must not minimize the importance of our own character.

Just as there are leadership types, there are also leadership styles that we must explore as we think about how our personality, choices, and interactions impact others, especially those who we serve. For these purposes, it is worth noting that one's leadership style has to do with the manner and approach of providing direction, including laying out plans and relating with people as a leader. In 1939, a group of psychologists led by Dr. Kurt Lewin carried out the first major study on leadership styles. As a result of their research findings, they established three dominant styles: Authoritarian/Autocratic Style, Participative/Democratic Style, and Delegative/Laissez-faire Style (Lewin, K., Lippitt, R., & White, R. K., 1999/1939).

Since Lewin's original study, numerous leaders have expanded upon these styles, especially as it relates to organizational leadership in business. Anita Campbell (2016) of Small Business Trends, LLC is often cited as a subject matter expert when it comes to leadership styles. Her work reminds us that who we are as leaders is equally as important as how we lead: "Being an effective leader is one essential part of running a successful business. But there isn't just one right way to be a great leader. You can choose and develop a leadership style that works for you, your team and your business goals"("Effective Leadership Styles in Business," para. 5). As such, it is worth taking a closer look at the three most dominant leadership styles and thinking about how they apply to your trajectory as a leader.

Authoritarian/Autocratic Style

This is a style that involves leaders telling their followers what to do without involving them in the decision-making process. It is leader-centric. The leader decides what he/she wants to do and also decides the way they want it accomplished without seeking any input or advice from their teammates or followers. This is more or less like giving a command or order and expecting others to follow.

Some people use this opportunity to treat their team members badly, ordering them around like servants. Some even go so far as yelling or calling others derogatory names. This is no longer leadership but tyranny, a display of an immature character, and Dwight Eisenhower (2013) has rightly said that, "You do not lead by hitting people over the head-that's assault, not leadership" (as cited in Kisel, para. 3).

It should be noted that the authoritarian style should rarely be used, if ever, unless it is the only means for one to encourage cooperation and teamwork from the team members. For instance, a leader can use the authoritative style with a new employee or team member who is learning about the new job. In this case, the leader serves as a coach and guide for the new teammate, and this boosts the confidence, knowledge and experience of the new person.

As time goes on, the leader can begin to ask for the opinion of the team member based upon the experience that he/she has had. This style of leadership can also be used when there is not enough time to make a decision and it has to be made quickly, for instance during an emergency. The leader can then make a lone decision to meet up and save time. (Lewin, K., Lippitt, R., & White, R. K., 1999/1939).

Participative/Democratic Style

This leadership style involves the leader including the team members in a decision-making process. However, the leader still makes the final decisions but with influence from the team members. This is done when the leader has a part of the information required and the employees or teammates have the other parts. The leader establishes the fact that he/she is not an island of knowledge and they respect the input of their teammates. This creates a mutual benefit for all stakeholders, as both the leader and followers have a say in the decision-making process. This also suggests that a leader must develop their teammates to the point of trusting them enough to take pieces of advice from them. Respect is established and cooperation is encouraged (Lewin, K., Lippitt, R., & White, R. K., 1999/1939).

Delegative/Laissez-Faire Style

This style is also known as free-reign; it means that the overwhelming number of the decisions made are derived from the team members, although there is still an amount of input from the leader. This is done when the employees or teammates have the ability to analyze the present situation; they know what needs to be done and how to get something completed. This shows that the leader has enough confidence in their teammates to allow them to make most of the decisions. However, this is not an avenue to blame the employees or team members when something goes wrong or expected outcomes are not met.

The delegative leadership style does not mean that the leader is weak or incapable. It rather shows respect and confidence for one's teammates; as such, there will be better cooperation and great team work. The free reign style can also be used when the leader is not around and there is a decision to be made. This will automatically be entrusted in the hands of capable employees or team members. It points to a fact that a leader ought to know, to a reasonable degree, his/her employees or teammates in terms of experience, knowledge, capability, in addition to having the ability to determine their weak points and strong points.

A good leader uses a combination of all three styles, depending on the situation. In addition, there are some factors that will determine what style is best to be used in certain situations. One should consider:

➢ The amount of time that is available.

➢ Whether the leader has respect or trust for the employees/team members.

➢ The person who has the necessary information, whether the leader, team member(s) is one of them.

➢ The knowledge, experience, capability of the employees or team members. Are they vastly knowledgeable or just learning?

➢ The amount of stress involved for the leader and/or the members of the team. One will definitely have to relieve the other by helping out.

➢ The type of task that needs to be done. Is it simple or complicated task (requiring both the leader and team members)?

➢ How well do the leader and team members get along? Is there conflict or not?

Your answer to these questions will serve as the catalyst for the actions that are required. It is worth noting that various circumstances that a leader encounters will determine the leadership style that must be adopted to yield favorable outcomes. My experiences have led me to believe that a wise and good leader will not stick to just one style. He/she will be flexible, as to the best style to be adopted depending on the situation at hand, the level of urgency and the desired outcomes. This shows that such a leader is wise and ready to bend and make the best out of their leadership, demonstrating that the leader has sound leadership strength (Lewin, K., Lippitt, R., & White, R. K., 1999/1939).

Chapter 3

THE CONCEPT OF LOVE

"Love is that condition in which the happiness of another person is essential to your own."

-Robert A. Heinlein

"Forget about me. I love you. My happiness isn't determined by my actions; my happiness is determined by your happiness. I get happy knowing that you are happy." When I stated this on the *Ellen DeGeneres Show*, I meant every single word. More than rhetoric and definitely not hyperbole, these words were spoken from the heart. Over time, as a man, father, principal, and leader, I have learned that the concept of love, often forgotten and ignored, is the most important concept to not only embrace, but to live every day.

There are many places upon which we can begin to explore the meaning of love. Some of us may draw from ancient texts; others may look to popular culture and yet others may rely exclusively upon our own experiences and expectations. I'd like to anchor this discussion in Merriam-Webster's (2020) definition that love is: "1) a strong affection for someone arising from kinship or personal ties (e.g. maternal love for a child), or 2) affection based on admiration, benevolence or common interests"(para. 1).

The second definition leads us to the real meaning of love in respect to transforming organizational leadership. Leadership that anchors love can be thought of as a form of love leadership; it is the affection that is based on the selfless love described by the Greeks as agape. It is often embodied and practiced by great leaders from a diverse range of industries; it is the kind of love a leader should have towards his/her followers. In the timeless words of the late rapper Heavy D (1989), this sentiment can be captured by the phraseology, "I got nothing but love for you baby." But, what exactly do we mean when we say that love should anchor our roles as leaders?

As with most words, to truly understand it, we need to explore its origins. The word "love" is deeply rooted in the English language. It was coined from the old English words *lufu* and *leof* which are also similar to the old German word luba. All of these words mean one thing, 'dear'. Other words related to the word love are lubere or libere. Accordingly, these are Roman words and they mean *to please*.

Greek philosophers, in particular, are credited with identifying and categorizing different types of love. They identified various types of love that we still use today when describing human relationships. They are: Eros/Erotic love, Philia/Affectionate love, Storge/Familiar love,

Ludus/Playful love, Mania/Obsessive love, Pragma/Enduring love, Philautic/Self-love and Agape/Selfless love. Each of these types of love have distinctive characteristics as outlined below. Each one also has implications for transforming organizational leadership.

1. **Eros/Erotic love:** This is the first kind of love, and it is named after the Greek god of love and fertility 'Eros.' The god Eros represents the idea of sexual passion and desire.

2. **Philia/Affectionate love**: This second type of love is that of friendship. It is valued above Eros as it signifies love between equals.

3. **Storge/Familiar love:** This love is similar to Philia, with one significant difference—it is a natural form of affection that mostly exists between parents and their children and vice versa.

4. **Ludus/Playful love:** This love is a bit similar to Eros but much more than that. The Greeks thought of Ludus as a playful form of love. It is represented as a kind of affection between young lovers. This is the early stage of falling in love with someone.

5. **Mania/Obsessive love:** This type of love is the one that addicts experience either from drugs, sex, or other items that one can get addicted to.

6. **Pragma/Enduring love:** This love is the kind that has aged and creates a unique bond has been formed over time. That type of love is mostly found in married couples or long-term friends.

7. **Philautic/Self-love:** This form of love is the type an individual has for his/her self. This is not an unhealthy type of love but one that allows an individual to see himself for who she/he is

and accept it.

8. **Agape/Selfless love:** This is the highest form of love. It is when one loves someone unconditionally and readily sacrifices for that person. This is the type of love that great leaders portray. It is selfless.

With a clearer understanding of the types of love, leaders can explore the features of love that directly affect their organizations and their corporate culture. Understandably, there are several features of love, but the main ones include: respect, trust, communication, selflessness, and teamwork. In order to truly integrate the concept of love into your work as a leader, it is important to understand how all of these variables anchor your manifestation of leading with love.

Respect

Like most words in the English dictionary, the word respect was coined from the Latin word *respectus* which means attraction, regard or consideration. In this context, respect is defined as an act of valuing and honoring a person in total, including valuing someone's words, actions, and feelings. Respect is a very important ingredient in any type of relationship especially when people have to work together towards common goals or outcomes. Yet, it is important to note that respect is not a singular, all-inclusive, term. There are several types of respect as outlined below:

➢ **Self-respect**: This is a form of respect that an individual has for themselves. They appreciate, value, and accept what they have and who they are.

➤ **Respect for others**: This is when someone accepts and values someone other than themselves. Richard Branson states that, "Respect is how to treat everyone."

➤ **Respect for social rules**: This is the obeying of and complying to rules and regulations that govern a particular society.

➤ **Respect for nature**: Appreciating all that nature has to offer and preserving it anyway possible is a sign of respect.

In a nutshell, if you have respect for yourself and others, you will also be respected.

Trust

Trust is the act of totally believing the words of someone you trust knowing and hoping you won't get lied to. In a *Harvard Business Review* article titled, "How Trustworthy Are You?" John Baldoni (2008) contends that: "Trust is essential to leadership. A truism indeed" (para. 1). Trust is also defined as a state of emotional vulnerability. This emotion is really needed for any kind of relationship to succeed, whether it is a romantic or business relationship. One thing that some people fail to understand is that trust is not forced but rather, it is gained. It doesn't automatically mean that because you're a parent to the person, your child must trust you. You have to earn someone else's trust. There are several forms of trust depending on the type of rapport that one is in. For example, fidelity is a form of love that is expected to be found in a romantic relationship, but in the context of leadership, we have:

- **Physical safety**
- **Financial trust**
- **Truthfulness**
- **Reliability**

- **Physical safety:** It is a very important form of trust and is termed to be the highest form of safety. If anyone can trust you with their physical safety, they definitely can trust you with their life. There are even some people that don't trust their leaders with anything, let alone their lives! Therefore, it is very important to make your team members trust you enough to be able to feel safe when they are with you.

- **Financial trust:** What kind of relationship is it if team members can't trust their leader with anything that has to do with finances? An inability to trust in this area leads to a faulty relationship because it means your team members do not trust your judgement on anything concerning money. Learn to put your team members first as you're now a team leader because without trust, that relationship is problematic.

- **Truthfulness:** This is an act of always saying the truth no matter which situation you find yourself in. Always learn to tell your team members the truth, even if it may be to reprimand them. Doing this will make them better people. Let your team members know that they can always hear the hard truth from you and telling the truth reflects your character and integrity.

➢ **Reliability**: Let your team members know that they can always depend on you. Your relationship doesn't always have to be official and cold. Let them be free enough to talk to you about their problems. Sometimes, it may not be financial help they need but just someone who will listen to whatever is bothering them. This doesn't make you look cheap; it only makes you human. It shows your compassion and reliability (Baldoni 2008).

Communication

This is a cornerstone of forming healthy and productive relationships with your peers and those whom you lead. Communication simply means being able to talk and listen to another person. Think of some of your most important relationships—how successful would they be if communication were not centered? As such, communication is needed for a leadership relationship. In the team of people who you're leading, you will see several people with different personalities. Therefore, it will be advisable to learn the art of communication with them so as to understand each other. Also, know this fact: you're not always right. Therefore, always welcome opinions from all of them. It is not every time that you will know what to do. Always ask for ideas from them: this makes them feel useful and important. The main objective of communication is to find a level ground.

Selflessness

I'd like to return to the quote that anchors this chapter: Forget about me. I love you. My happiness isn't determined by my actions; my happiness is determined by your happiness. I get happy knowing that you are happy. One of the reasons why I was, and I still am, able to say this is because it is the truth. My desire to see my students happy is anchored in altruism—it is a selfless belief that their well-being is important. Such a belief is not derived from my gaining anything tangible or intangible in return—it is selfless.

Too often in our modern society, we, even as leaders, put ourselves first. This can lead to conflict, selfish actions and self-serving decisions. However, when we put others first, we can see a different realm of possibilities.

1. **It improves relationships**: Whether it's friendship, parent-child, or business, this applies to every relationship. By committing selfless acts for those we care about, we are showing them how true our love is because selflessness can only be from love.

2. **It keeps us healthy**: Scientists suggest that selflessness has to do with inner-love, and inner-peace is an important factor involved in reducing the level of cortisol, which is the hormone that triggers cardiovascular disease. Therefore, being selfless reduces your chances of having a heart attack. Interestingly, it is beneficial, in this case to the leader, in the sense that a leader who is not fit may not be in the position to lead, so good health is very

important.

3. **It forms a connection**: Acting selflessly bonds us with a lot of people, and when you help them, a connection is formed and you may become genuine friends.

4. **It gives you a sense of peace**: The fact that you're making others happy gives you joy and satisfaction and this in turn gives you peace.

Team Work

Teamwork is a very important feature of love. This is a collaborative effort of a group of people to achieve a common goal or to complete a task in the most efficient and effective way. Just like the saying goes "no man is an island," it shows that everyone needs help once in a while. It is worth noting that there are several significant aspects of teamwork. Some of them include:

-   **Productivity**: "Two heads are better than one." Although this is just as a saying, it is true. The work you get done all by yourself is not as productive as the work you get when you work together as a team. It doesn't matter whether you're the boss or not, the fact is that you can't know everything or do everything by yourself.

-   **Connection**: As you get to work together with your team members, you learn more about them and get closer. During your working together, a bond is formed and this leads to friendship.

- **Sense of responsibility and belonging**: Being on a team gives each member a sense of belonging. No matter how small the input is, they all get to contribute in meaningful ways. This makes them feel important and gives them a sense of responsibility.

- **Conducive working environment**: When members of a team work together as one, it provides a peaceful environment for working. And when there is a peaceful environment, there is bound to be maximum output.

- **Provides great learning ability**: Working as a team helps us learn from our mistakes. And also, we gain insight and learn new concepts from more experienced colleagues (i.e. you expand your skills and gain more experience from members of your team).

Different perspectives: Teamwork provides the company with diverse thoughts, perspectives, opportunities and problem-solving approaches. A good teamwork structure gives individuals the opportunity to brainstorm collectively and, in turn, increases their success with solving problems and accomplishing goals (Moseley, 2020).

Chapter 4

WHEN LOVE AND LEADERSHIP MEET

"The giving of love is an education itself."

-Eleanor Roosevelt

The academic school years of 2019-2020 and 2020-2021 reflect the importance of why leadership and love must be more than just buzz words or trends. Like most people, I never imagined that I'd be a school leader in the midst of a global pandemic. Leading a school of over 600 students, 99% of whom are students of color and who qualify for reduced or free lunch, the pandemic has illuminated that doing 'business as usual' just will not work.

Because love is centered in our leadership practices and our entire leadership team embraces it, we had to look at innovative ways to service our students and their families. With many of them neither having access to Wi-Fi at home nor having access to personal computers, we had to ensure that whether in-person or online, our scholars did not stop learning. Because we love them, we knew that our concern for them couldn't just be about the bottom line—we had to embrace and service the whole child. This meant partnering with Wi-Fi providers, getting students access to computers, and making sure that they received hot meals. It is the latter that most people may not think about.

In a school where most of our children are at/below the federal poverty line, it means that many of them will go without food if school is not open. Many of their parents may work multiple jobs which means that they are not in a position to stay at home to provide meals or even provide supervision for their children. Therefore, without their school family stepping in, these children and their families would have found themselves in a precarious position—both being hungry and getting further behind academically.

A traditional leadership model might say that issues like these are the concerns of the families, social workers, religious organizations and/or social services; however, when love and leadership meet, it means that this problem is not a problem. Instead, it is a solution waiting to happen. And that is exactly what we are doing—providing a solution by partnering with local restaurants, food suppliers, and those who have experience working in food deserts. We are making sure that even when the brick and mortar school is not in session, our students are still provided with hot meals. Yes, their education is our primary charge, but can we ignore the other variables that factor into their lives and impact their ability to learn? No!

As illustrated here, leading with love is knowing and caring about what inspires and empowers people. It is caring enough to know what is of importance to them. To help them succeed is to lead with love because it will also help you succeed. It works both ways: it gives satisfying results of having reached your potential and goal. Accordingly, Robert A Heinlein (2013) states, "Love is that condition in which the happiness of another person is essential to your own" (as cited in Philosiblog, para 1).

Being a leader who leads with love helps you to help people achieve more than they ever thought they could. It also helps you to think outside of the box. No matter how long you have been in a leadership position, nothing should be so predictable that you are not prepared. Loving while leading helps to nudge someone in the right direction towards self-discovery, setting and attaining lofty heights/goals, personal accountability, and learning persistence while also encouraging them to do the same to others.

As we reflect upon these goals, we must also consider how the advancement of technology is having a great impact on how work is done or carried out in various workplaces. As I mentioned at the beginning of this chapter, the digital divide is real. Yet, this is not just a reality for school-age children. Globalization means that today's workforce must be prepared to compete and they must be willing to learn new practices and skills in order to remain competitive. As leaders, it is our job to make sure that those whom we serve are prepared and it starts with us.

Essentials of Leading with Love

As mentioned in the introduction, the essence of this book is to clearly explore the importance of leading in love. Sacrificial love in this world of ours cannot be discarded because it is essentially what we need. Although normally, the leader is seen as being directly responsible for causing a change, sometimes the methods of achieving this are authoritative. This model of leadership is not democratic nor is it aligned with the premise of focusing on incorporating love in your leadership.

Historically, leaders are more productive when the emotion of love is incorporated in their leadership style. Although the autocratic leader may forcefully command respect on the part of the followers, they eventually cause their followers to revolt against them. Although there are increasing societal pressures and demands that undermine leaders because of a push for productivity, high test scores, or maximized profit margin, this should not discourage aspiring or seasoned leaders from the practice of leading in love. Instead, the idea of leadership not grounded in love should inspire all of us even more. And that inspiration is directly linked to thinking outside of the box. As we are reminded in the article "Leadership as an Act of Love: Leading in Dangerous Times" by Mónica C. Byrne-Jiménez and Irene H. Yoon (2019), "Freedom is made of dreams, and dreams help us transgress what already exists. Imagination is transcendent, while being equal parts rebellious and visionary. When we imagine, as leaders, we draw on our other habits of the heart. It takes courage and wisdom to figure out how to dream, how to build" (p. 18).

Individuals who develop the attitude of incorporating the ethics of love into their daily undertakings and permitting them to control and change how they reason and do things, are aware of how their presence influences other people. They begin to attract and keep like-minded people on their team, or what I referred to previously as "matching your fly." Conversely, organizations with high attrition rates tend to be unstable—a constant shift in personalities and energies will not help your organization grow. Instead, you will find yourself constantly in retool, pause, or even start-over mode. Stagnation will become your kryptonite.

Because of this, I tell my team to constantly think outside of the box. We should not just follow the typical ways common to other schools, organizations, or districts; instead, we should show a great commitment to discovering ways of bringing love in view to the consciousness of those whom we serve. In turn, all leaders need to establish a balance on how to impact all without necessarily neglecting any one person on the team. This may require taking a bold step to explore what leadership focusing on love could look like in your business or organization. As we have uncovered, it begins with the little unnoticed selflessness we display to the people around us. So, for every boy, girl, man, or woman on the streets you were able to help but did nothing about it, you've just denied such a person the opportunity of being loved. More importantly, indirectly, you denied yourself the honor of being a leader by the example of love. The rules are simple, more often than not: when we seek to be served rather than serve, we don't exhibit the tenets of love. Every leader is saddled with the obligation of service. They are to make a positive change and set a benchmark of love and service for all to follow.

Just in the schools where I have served, I have noticed that there are many people around us suffering from traumatizing conditions, neurological disorders, life-threatening ailments, social, emotional, intellectual challenges because of constant subjection to poverty, systemic racism, residential volatility, immigration, hunger, hostility, and delinquency by the court systems. All of these are problems looking for solutions and great leaders see problems not as hurdles, but as opportunities to give.

The Quintessential Love

In the Byrne-Jiménez and Yoon article (2019), the authors acknowledge that leadership can no longer be about the search for a "theory of everything" or a set of static "best practices" (p. 117). Leadership is about love and active love is a verb. It requires some movement or motion. You cannot passively engage in active love. Leaders who are determined to transform the lives of others understand that love is, therefore, a reflection of our humanity.

Similarly, in the book, *Strength to Love* (1963, 2010), Martin Luther King Jr. argues that "the ultimate measure of a man is not where he stands in moments of comfort and convenience but where he stands at times of challenge and controversy"(p. 26). Within this context, the notion of love relies upon one having a connection with humanity and a willingness to be courageous in the face of adversity, even if it means being an outlier. This, I believe, is the quintessential element of love within an organizational context.

It is of the belief that love is like a vigor that originates from our inside to defend and care for others. Since it proceeds from within us, we should be careful so as not to take it for granted and misuse it. Love takes the highest risks ever but ensures it protects and preserves others. This serves to motivate us to have goals beyond the present and never allow mind limitations but debunk the heart of limits and develop in body, mind, and spirit. Love is much easier when it is reciprocal and not one-sided. Love is wise yet very flexible although it also passes through pains with others but heals by grace. It becomes stronger when it is certain that disappointment brings strength. Love is unhappy with segregation and injustice but keeps preaching resistant to hatred. Love, often lowered to the secluded domain, comes to light in the leadership and relationships of people and their families. Love is the public nature of love and loving that elevates it as a way of leading and a purpose for leadership. Love is powerful because it integrates the personal and the public, especially in the service to children.

We saw this firsthand when we started implementing washing machines and dryers in the school. One morning, a young lady came to school. As we were checking her bag in, she threw a bottle of water at one of the security guards. A scuffle ensued and we ended up detaining her. We later found out that the young lady was ashamed that she had dirty clothes in her bag. She did not want anyone to know. Here she was homeless, yet, she thought enough of her education that she still came to school. I knew then that we had to do something.

Like most urban leaders, I know that poverty is sometimes a stain that others judge with disdain. It can lead to shame, fear, or a lack of self-esteem. Coupled with social media and the tendency for some kids to tease other kids who they perceive as different, I did not want any of my students feeling as if something that they could not control made them less than. My team and I decided that if dirty clothes were the problem, we'd implement washing machines and dryers and we would even clean the clothes for our students. After going through a few logistical and political hurdles, we made washing our students' clothes a reality. We knew that we had to take tangible steps to show them that we loved them and cared. We knew that leadership involved a love exemplified by care, respect, and responsibility as articulated by bell hooks in her seminal works (1994, 2001). Leadership focused on love means choosing to be truly present with those in need to serve them and facilitate in the building, and creation of emotional and intellectual areas to which everyone can benefit, especially the society.

Transformational leadership is not capricious; it is not whimsical or fleeting; it is an active habit that transforms a community into one that is focused on the greater good of that community. We not only cleaned clothes, but we transformed the lives of our children and their families.

Chapter 5

7 TRANSFORMATIONAL STEPS TOWARDS LEADING WITH LOVE

As leaders, it is imperative that we make a real effort to understand each other. Working in diverse workplaces with colleagues from diverse backgrounds can make communicating a challenge. We only need to look at our relationships outside of work—with our parents, our children, or our partners—to know that even if we are spending a considerable amount of time together, it's still hard to truly understand one another. It helps to assume that, most of the time, our colleagues have good intentions and to acknowledge that those good intentions can sometimes be quite literally lost in translation.

This gets easier if we foster a deep sense of wonder and curiosity in our relationships which allows us to become genuinely interested in our colleagues. This is accomplished by listening deeply to what they are saying (and to what they are not saying), asking lots of questions, and exploring their perspectives from all angles. Judging and blaming are easy and just as easily lead to disengagement and conflict. On the other hand, staying open and curious in conversations generates an environment where people feel heard, seen, and truly cared about. In this chapter, I will explore seven transformational steps that will set you on the path to leading with love.

Step 1: Understanding the Value of Weaknesses

As a basketball player, my size and athleticism made me better suited to play basketball than to play soccer. Although both are sports that require speed, agility, and quick-thinking, I gravitated towards the sport that best suited my strengths. Just like sports, as leaders, we tend to lean towards those things that make us more successful; yet, we can't forget that there is value in understanding our weaknesses.

It is fair to say that no one is good at everything and everyone makes mistakes; yet, our natural tendency is to hide our failures and cover our weaknesses. In intimate relationships, our flaws are only too visible to our partners. Feeling accepted despite our shortcomings increases our own tolerance for the mistakes of others and builds our generosity for forgiving them. It's no different at work. The key for focusing on the love is to nurture a culture where people feel safe enough to be vulnerable. Vulnerability is one of those qualities we first look for in others, but is the last thing we want to show ourselves. Yes, being vulnerable takes courage. We need to know that we can ask our colleagues for help when we are struggling and that we will be supported when things go wrong. Yes, we will get feedback and are expected to learn from it, but we will not be rejected for making a mistake. Vulnerability is also one of those qualities we first look for in others but is the last thing we want to show ourselves.

Step 2: Engage in Thoughtful Dialogue

As a school leader, I've had some difficult conversations with staff, teachers, parents, and peers. No one likes to deliver the bad news or be perceived as the bad guy. Yet, effective leadership requires courage and that courage will require you to engage in thoughtful and sometimes, difficult dialogue. When we are willing to challenge those around us to optimize their skill set and talents, it translates into a win-win.

No personal or professional relationship is free from rocky junctures and most of us want to walk away from addressing conflict (and there are a million ways in which we do this). If we are willing to knowingly walk into difficult conversations that require us to show up fully, we can both work on the issues and improve the way we relate to each other. As leaders, courageous conversations are so difficult because they play both on our anxiety to upset the other person as well as on our fear of not handling the conversation well and being rejected ourselves. We need to go into these conversations with unconditional positive regard for the person sitting across from us and be prepared for real emotional engagement. A courageous conversation blends mercy and truth, and it requires and creates tenderness. If done well, it builds stronger connections.

Step 3: Embrace that Leadership Is All About Love, Not Power

There is a popular show called *Power* on one of the premium cable channels, Starz. The show centered on the age-old premise that people will do anything to gain power or take power away from someone else. It is a storyline as old as time and can be traced back to the book of Genesis in the Torah and the Bible. It is such a pervasive way of thinking about leadership that, even today, too many people conflate leadership with power. I argue that true leadership is all about love.

Infusing the kind of love that I have described throughout this book into our workplaces is more than just a humane thing to do. My experiences show me that people who work in a culture where they feel free to express affection, tenderness, care, and compassion for one another are more satisfied with their jobs, committed to the organization, and accountable for their performance. I intentionally and frequently check in with my teachers and staff. I want to know how things are going and I want them to process how they fit into our larger mission and goal to service our children and their families. My role, in part, is to prepare them to lead.

Nee-Benham et al. (1998) described leaders' commitment to the "public process of loving, of behaving in a loving manner" as transformational (p. 145). When we think about it, schools are microcosms of society. Accordingly, most young people are first exposed to diverse leadership models at school. If pre-K through 12th grade students saw adults as exemplars of love and not just authoritarians, how different might our communities be? My point is that seeing love as a springboard for learning can become normative. We, within the education community, can create a model for other leaders as to how to lead with purpose, especially in light of other societal problems that young people face.

Step 4: Practice What is in Your Heart

Love as an active form of leadership may seem to challenge the current state of education. With local, state, and federal policies that often use test scores to determine growth and merit, it may seem daunting to do more than what is required. Yet, as leaders, we must. Let me, briefly, return to the story about our implementing washers and dryers at the school. Once we received both some local and international attention, we started to receive laundry detergent, softeners, and other supplies from all around the world. Before we knew it, we had a surplus of supplies. Our students were getting their clothes cleaned and many started to beam with pride knowing that they did not have to come to school with dirty clothes on. Through our focus on the love, we taught them life skills and removed a barrier to their academic outcomes.

Yet, as leaders, we knew that we could do even more. We did not engage in self-congratulatory praises; instead, we started thinking about other, tangible concerns that we needed to address. We launched a school store where we offered other hygiene products for both young women and young men. As their principal, I was also their protector. As a practice of the heart, I had to remove barriers—even the ones that were not directly tied to academics or education. Like most leaders, I have to contend with internal and external factors. Whether it is from our central office and policy makers to our parents and community leaders. Understandably, most leaders—regardless of one's industry—endure some strain and stress as an outgrowth of their leadership position. Yet, bell hooks (2009) reminds us that there is great value in being what she calls, "heartwhole" (p. 217). The heart, embodied by acts of love, is the foundation of a culture, a community. Furthermore, bell hooks argues that our educational system, in particular, can create a "language of healing, of hope, a language of dreams, a language of belonging" (p. 223).

Step 5: Have Courage

My relationship with my team, students, and family is anchored in love. It is not something that I am afraid to share. In fact, I am proud to share it because too often we do not have the courage to talk about the value that love adds to our roles as leaders. We must be courageous enough to take risks, to challenge the status quo, and to remember for whom we are fighting and serving. This all stems from having authentic relationships which require transparency and courage, the courage to say and mean, "I love you."

Because love thrives through connection, courage is made possible when organizational leaders experience collective joy. It can be something as simple as making sure that our educational spaces are responsive, creative, and playful for adults and students. These moments fuel leaders' abilities to stay courageous on behalf of those in their communities. Yet, it is worth noting that courageous love does not equate mediocrity. Some mistakenly believe that love and leadership can lead to weakness or a lack of respect. This, unfortunately, is due to how we have come to think about love. Instead of seeing it as a superpower, we see it as an Achilles' heel. Perhaps this is why some believe when leadership is courageous, it is less difficult. The opposite is true. The courage that is needed to lead with love is the springboard for dream making and catching—your dreams, your team's dreams, and other stakeholders' dreams. It is only a lack of innovation, creativity, and imagination that prevent us from having the courage to lead with love.

Step 6: Seek Wisdom in Unconventional Places

If we only think of wisdom as book knowledge or a formal education, we are missing the point. Wisdom is often derived from lived experiences—those things that make us unique. Just as wisdom can be gained over time, it can be manifested in numerous ways. We gain wisdom by both doing and listening. Although the former is privileged in our society, I want to hone in on the latter—listening.

Any given day at West Side High School, I am in listening mode. From our cafeteria staff and security guard to my assistant principals and teachers, I am actively listening to their concerns, suggestions, and general feedback. Conventional wisdom might suggest that since I am the school's leader, there is not much that I can gain. However, because I respect every person at every level on my team, I recognize that a hierarchical approach to leading is not advantageous. Every adult on the team has a particular body of knowledge and specific skill sets that we all can benefit for. As a leader, it is my job to be available, accessible, and approachable. From this, I am able to gain wisdom that translates into a stronger organization and culture.

Step 7: Let Your Imagination Guide You

In the face of intense violence and discrimination, Martin Luther King Jr. had the audacity to imagine a different kind of world that acknowledged everyone's dreams as important and equally valued. He, like so many others, desired to see America uphold her promise of freedom for all of its citizens. Literary icon James Baldwin (1961, 2020) also reminded us over and over that to be a person of color,

> . . .and to be relatively conscious is to be in a state of rage almost, almost all of the time — and in one's work. And part of the rage is this: It isn't only what is happening to you. But it's what's happening all around you and all of the time in the face of the most extraordinary and criminal indifference…(as cited in *To Be in a Rage, Almost All the Time*, para. 2).

Both of these men used their platforms to carve out voices for Black Americans. They dared to imagine the world, not as it was, but as it could be. Thus is the role of a leader, regardless of one's industry, race, gender and/or socio-economic background. Even if we do not have the most desirable situation or the support of others, we can still imagine how things could be.

Because of this, I do believe that each of us has the power to transform the lives of others. When we magnify that times millions, it becomes clear why the imagination is so critical. In fact, the Lights On Program reflects what can happen when imagination and reality collide to create something impactful.

Most studies show that young people are most likely to get in trouble after school and during the evening hours, especially if an adult is not at home (Halpern, 1999). If young people remain unsupervised without something positive to do, there is a great likelihood that they will be attracted to activities for which they can get in trouble. Although school lets out in the early afternoon, I knew that it was inexcusable to believe that once the final bell rang, our jobs were over. Using a little ingenuity and a lot of imagination, I created the Lights On Program that kept the school open beyond school hours. Students could stay warm, be in a safe environment surrounded by loving adults, and receive a free meal. Without the burden and stress of worrying about where their children were, many parents saw this program as a true lifesaver. Like so many of the initiatives that we see in business and schools, this one all started because we dared to dream of an alternative to our current reality.

Chapter 6

ULTIMATE THOUGHTS ON
LEADERSHIP AS LOVE

The seventh step in the previous chapter revolves around the imagination. It is the failure of imagination that will sometimes prevent us from being the leaders that we were called to be. Think about it in pragmatic terms: All realities first started as dreams. The Notorious B.I.G., perhaps, said it best: "It was all a dream." When we fail to dream, we fail to see the possibility or the *yet* that can still happen. When we, as leaders, do not encourage those around us to dream, we miss out on new concepts, ideas, innovations, and solutions. Our shortsightedness can minimize our success. This is why my previous discussion about "Match my fly" is so important. You set the tone, the climate, and the culture. As leaders, our job is to build, grow, and help enhance the lives of those around us.

In discussing leadership in this capacity, I've drawn from my experiences in a school setting; yet, it is worth noting that these concepts, ideas, and steps can be applied in any industry. Ask yourself: How is my role as a leader anchored in love? What do I do that reflects a love of my team? How is love reflected by those whom we serve?

The answers to these questions will vary depending on where you are on your leadership journey. Yet, they are helpful in helping you to see how the ideas expressed in this book align with your current leadership style and practices. Leaders are often called upon to make difficult decisions. In a best- case scenario, he/she will be received as doing the right thing; however, there are occasions where a leader will make a mistake and his/her decision does not lead to optimal results. If you are only in leadership for fame, fortune, glory, accolades, status, or power, your tenure will probably be short-lived. Although these tangibles are gratifying, they cannot be the only reasons to lead.

When you focus on the love, as I have contended throughout this book, you lead with purpose. A purpose-driven man or woman is powerful. Every day, leaders must choose between what is right and what is wrong; they must understand how their actions affect others and they must do so with an uncompromising belief in that which is right. We can't give up on those whom we serve. As I like to call my students, "We can't give up on our babies." When we do, we are ultimately giving up on our entire community and that, especially in today's climate, is not an option.

However, we must not pretend as if this is utopic and leaders have super powers, especially school leaders. School leaders are in a unique position because the overwhelming majority of our students are minors. As such, we cannot, nor should we, engage in the work that we do alone. Education is a business that is often driven by larger systems which create and dictate leadership infrastructures. Yet, this should not stop us from taking risks even if those risks scare us.

What Love Does

When I was first approached about going to West Side as an assistant principal, I was, admittedly, skeptical because of the reports that I heard about what happened in and around the school. It was not uncommon to hear West Side referred to as 'the Bermuda triangle.' Some people would say that like the legendary triangle, "Stuff went in and didn't come out."

As there are in many impoverished and underserved communities of color, there were regular incidents of violence and gang operations. Understandably, parents didn't want their kids attending such a school. Like most parents, why wouldn't parents from the Newark community want more? I knew and I understood. Yet, I also saw potential for even more, and this was driven by love.

One of my first incidents at the school was both tragic and emblematic of my students' lives. They were young in age, but many dealt with trauma. One of my students was killed and left decomposing in an abandoned building because she was pregnant. I remember how indifferent and disinterested the majority of my students were. Others were, understandably, afraid. I could not let that fear permeate the entire school. If I did, it would create a culture of fear and distrust.

Like many of the examples that I referenced previously in the book, I knew that I had to come up with something quick enough to keep my students in school. I needed them engaged, interested, and ready to learn. As a leader, I had to put aside any of my distractions and doubts because my team needed me focused and prepared to lead. I knew that coming across in an authoritative manner was not the best approach. They didn't need a Joe Clark from the movie *Lean on Me.*

I also knew that they didn't need someone to judge them. They were young and they were vulnerable, so I had to try something different—love. We showered them with love; we reassured them that they were safe; we helped them understand that we cared for them, and we would do everything in our power to keep them safe inside and outside of school. From there, we were able to really focus on students who were serious about learning. We wanted them to feel fully vested in and capable of being successful regardless of their neighborhood or home environment.

What Does Love-in-Action Look Like?

Love inspires performance excellence and resilience.

Serving others is a reflection of love. Research described in Adam Grant's book *Give and Take: Why Helping Others Drives Our Success* (2013) states that, "Givers succeed in a way that creates a ripple effect, enhancing the success of people around them (p. 10). As a principal, I notice that high school teachers who believe they are making a difference are less likely to burnout than those who don't. The most effective leaders inspire people by connecting them with the people they serve to show them how the work they do is helping others.

Love Pulls People Together.

Taking time to get to know and care for the people you lead brings about greater unity. This unity is especially important as your team faces adversity. When love exists among the members of a group, they are more likely to pull together than to tear one another apart. The bond or connection they feel helps them overcome the inevitable obstacles every organization encounters.

Love Overlooks Minor Offenses.

When love is present in a team, department, or organization, people are more likely to assume the best in others and give them the benefit of the doubt. For example, if a colleague says something that is irritating or hurtful, leading with love means that one is inclined to cut them some slack. The absence of love, potentially offending words or deeds are more likely to bring about retaliation and sprout rivalries that undermine performance.

Love Reduces Stress.

No job should be so detrimental that it impacts your physical or mental well-being. Love among the members of a group serves as a protective factor from chronic stress so that people are healthier and better able to perform at the top of their game.

Chapter 7

CREATING POSITIVE CULTURE IN YOUR ORGANIZATION

Think of the worst job that you have ever had. What role did the leadership play in your experience? Did you trust the leader? Did you respect him/her? Were you able to approach the leader?

More than likely a lack of trust and respect contributed to your poor work experience. Now that you are a leader, how do you use those negative experiences to motivate yourself and others around you?

As with any leadership role, being self-reflective, process-oriented, and honest in your approach will provide you with both moments of clarity and much needed introspection. In reflecting backwards and planning forward, we begin to see not just the larger vision, but the specific details about how we lead and who we are as leaders. A leader who is not willing to look inward is probably not a good leader after all.

I have learned that three tenets—understanding your organization, understanding love as a commitment and understanding love as a gift—

can help you transform any environment, even one that is deemed as failing or undesirable. Once I began to understand how important these tenets were, I was able to intentionally cultivate a family-like culture. Over time, I saw things improve and that improvement helped me to carve out a leadership model that can be replicated at other schools and within other industries.

TENET ONE: Understanding Your Organization

We should not associate death with youth, but in any urban environment from L.A. and Chicago to Newark and Miami, young people are killed tragically every day. To ignore this or pretend that it doesn't exist is a failure of leadership. As a leader, you must know the intricacies of your organization, even if they are difficult to face.

For me, tragedy has been a part of my tenure as school leader. Tragedy struck my first year when midway into the school year, another one of my students was violently killed because he allegedly knew where "the good drugs" were and he refused to tell. Another young life was taken too soon and it was affecting our school community. I was deeply saddened and I knew that this version of West Side High School had to change. I needed to right the ship and save my babies.

I wish I could tell you that this was an outlier and that we didn't experience any more tragic deaths, but we did. Sadly, in the next year, another death was recorded. One of the students was killed by a drive-by shooting two weeks from his graduation. There were three students killed during just my first year of leadership. I could have decided that there was nothing that I could do and accept that this was the organization that I had to lead or I could begin to strategize ways to improve the organization. I decided upon the latter. I knew my organization well enough to understand the changes I could implement short-and long-term.

TENET TWO: Understanding Love as a Commitment

Throughout his book, *The Road Less Travelled*, M. Scott Peck (2003) defined love as "a commitment to the welfare, growth, and wholeness of either oneself or another person"(p. 92). This may sound idealistic and maybe even utopic, so you may be asking: What does this look like in tangible terms?

Previously, I briefly mentioned the Lights On Program. Now, I'd like to delve into this more in order to show how the "Love as a Commitment" tenet works. The idea of the program was to keep the school open Friday nights from 6 p.m.-11 p.m. because that was when all of the crime was happening in the area. I wanted to create a safe haven for my students. In the summer, we wanted the school to be open three nights a week. Collectively, we would not just keep the school physically opened, but, together with people who loved the kids more than their jobs, we would use the period as an avenue to make the students better by providing them with access to role models, a hearty meal, recreational activities, and a designated space where they could be safe.

Since the inception of the Lights On Program, there has been an average of 6200 volunteer hours each year of the program and we have serviced an average of 350 students a day. To date, we have not lost any more students to gun violence. Our continued success can be attributed, in part, to our desire to REVAMP the lives of our community members.

Relationship building with students and staff

Educational support through social and emotional growth

Victorious impact on SGOs

Assess and eliminate non-academic barriers

Measurable data driven results

Partnerships with community stakeholders

The key is that we've been saving lives and we've been showing other schools that this model can work. The Lights On Program's positive impact is based upon its ability to provide both recreational and enrichment activities that focus on a safe environment where students are able to develop healthy and strong relationships with their peers and community. In an environment where a safe environment can literally make the difference between life and death, the Lights On Program provides social and emotional support to the youth who participate in the program.

Providing students with a safe alternative to the streets prevented the kids from getting in trouble. We also understood that the activities needed to reflect the interests of our entire student population. In addition, to help and encourage the female students, we added recording studios, henna, eyelashes, jewelry making, and fashion design. As you can imagine, as more female students started to attend so did the males.

The point here is that we could not just say that there was a problem. We could not just complain about factors that were beyond our control. We had to show our students and the larger Newark community that we were serious. We were serious enough to make a commitment through love. Little did we know that by doing what came natural to us, we would receive an outpouring of support. Oprah Winfrey was so inspired by this act of love, after seeing us featured on CBS's *This Morning*, she came to the school and donated $500,000. This generous gift meant that we could keep the Lights On Program operating all summer.

Oprah's gift and the countless others serve as reminders that love is powerful. You can't underestimate the power of love. The love that Oprah gave to them coupled with people from all over the world made our kids feel a sense of pride. None of this would have been possible if we did not make a commitment to love. With the gifts, we were able to expand our programmatic efforts and offer additional entrepreneurial skills training.

TENET THREE: Understanding the Gift of Love

We cannot assume that everyone we encounter from our peers to those who serve on our teams have experienced love. In fact, some leaders may find that others have difficulty receiving leadership that is anchored in love. For this reason, we must see love not as a lofty goal but as a reasonable gift that all leaders are capable of giving.

This crystalized for me when I separated some students while they were brawling. It was intense and I found myself using my own body to shield a boy on the bottom of the pile from the indiscriminate blows that he was receiving from the others. Almost instinctively, I wrapped my arms around another young man and then pulled a different boy from the brawl, until, finally, the fight stopped. I was visibly upset and disappointed. Yet, I knew that fights and conflicts were a reality of the job. It was just a day in the life of a school principal in an urban district.

I remember in early 2020 when I was interviewed by Matt Stanmyre of *NJ.com*. He asked me about my leadership style. I explained that as the leader of the school, I knew that I had to be fully present. My students needed to see me. I couldn't hide in my office when a fight was going on or when something chaotic happened in the school. How would I look going to get on the phone and calling security? You crazy? I *am* security. And this is exactly what the gift of love is all about—fully giving and committing yourself to a love that is greater than self. In all organizations, our team members are watching us and taking mental notes about how we respond. When it becomes clear what the expectations are and why, others will buy in and help build out the vision.

I believe that anything is possible! I want my students and team members to know that anything is possible. I want them to experience a family-like environment where they know that they are valued and appreciated. For many of them who may be coming from stressful home environments, I want to lessen the burden and provide them with a chance to truly be children and young adults, and to experience the joy of youth and the privilege of naivete that their more affluent peers get to experience. The key is understanding that they do have real-world problems. We must acknowledge that, in spite of their problems, their lives have great value and their futures can be successful.

For any leader to successfully create a culture of success it starts with a willingness to understand the task at hand, commit to being a change agent, and leverage one's genuine love for others to make a tangible difference. The following is a non-exhaustive list that leaders can draw from as they embark upon leading with love.

Other Ways to Lead With Love:

1. Be involved in the welfare of your team members even outside of their work life, e.g. know the names of their spouses and kids.

2. Be supportive of any member of your team who needs it. Ordinary words may go a long way.

3. Give room for communication where team members are encouraged to discuss their problems with you. Do not give room for an atmosphere where one is seen as unapproachable, intimidating, or overbearing.

4. Mentor and coach, instead of criticizing.

5. Listen to their complaints and concerns and encourage suggestions and ideas.

6. Show appreciation: Encourage your team members by appreciating them when they go out of their way to invest more in the business. Acknowledge and celebrate their achievements and accomplishments. This will encourage others too. Healthy competition to be the best will occur.

Chapter 8

HOW FAR ARE YOU WILLING TO GO?
ALFONZO'S STORY

It is my hope that as we have embarked upon this leadership journey together, there are some things shared in this book that have inspired you, challenged you, and/or motivated you as a leader. From someone just starting out to someone who is in a senior leadership role, we must all think about the power of love and its ability to yield both tangible and intangible results. For me, understanding how this plays out in my everyday role is best captured by the story of Alfonzo Anderson.

Alfonzo, affectionately known as Zo or Pound, was brought to my attention his sophomore year. Alfonzo came in as this humble kid. He was a quiet kid, but he was also involved in one of Newark's gangs. Like most of my parents, none of us want to believe that those within our community are making poor decisions. Yet, through it all, his mother has always been his biggest advocate. From the day Zo's life intersected with mine, his mom has been with us every step of the way.

As some of us might say, "She doesn't play." An older mother, she was also raising Alfonzo's sister's younger kids. Yet, even with her best intentions, her son needed more.

No matter how far she moved away from this area or Pennington Court as it's called, Alfonzo would always find his way down bottom and back entrenched in that gang life. Alfonzo was a student and basketball player who showed great promise athletically and academically. He was equally committed to the streets and gang life in particular. Affiliation with a particular gang meant that he had obligations and responsibilities that went well beyond the scope of what most 16-year-olds had to do.

The magnetism of the streets was strong and they pulled Zo in, as they had so many of Newark's other young Black and Latino men. Without some form of intervention, I knew that Zo could have easily become a victim of the streets and a statistic tucked away in some government document.

Being an all-county basketball player meant that Alfonzo was good; he was a very good player. During his junior year, in particular, he averaged almost a triple double: 30 points, 15 assists, and 10 rebounds for large stretches of the season. This was amazing talent. Zo would even come to games, allegedly high, and he would still ball his butt off. Yet, we knew that he was not reaching his full potential. And when all of it was said and done, he didn't really have any offers by the conclusion of his senior year.

I knew that his potential would be squandered if he didn't get an opportunity to play at the next level, and I also knew that he couldn't just go to any program and thrive. So, I thought about my friend JT

Burton who I went to school with. He was a college coach. He said "my man Saulsberry is in Cheyenne, Wyoming, at LCCC, Laramie County Community College." I contacted the coaching staff and they told me, "All right, say no more."

They came to see Pound play. That game, Pound put on a show. As a result, they gave Pound a scholarship. We sent Pound out to Wyoming in August. It was a great send off. People, including members of our team, were even crying. For a while, I didn't hear anything. Because Pound is a quiet young man, I was not totally surprised by his silence. Then, I received a message: "Cook, I think Zo is about to leave. He's getting that itch. Can you do something?"

I knew that talking to Pound over the phone was not the solution, so I hopped on a plane, flew into Denver, and then drove the rest of the way to Cheyenne, Wyoming. When I arrived, Zo didn't have any sheets on the bed, nor any pillows. I looked around and thought: How are you even surviving out here?

But in the same light, Zo wasn't taking anything from anyone, literally. I recall asking him, "How are you even washing clothes and stuff?"

With an infectious smile, and a slow drawl, he responded, "Yo, Cook, man, I just go to the laundromat and when anybody comes in, I ask can I throw this item in there with yours? Can you give me some laundry detergent?"

Clearly he was being resourceful, but I wanted him to have his own, so I went on a Walmart run. With whatever resources he had, I didn't want him to spend his last on laundry. We got him everything that a college dorm should have.

In my heart, I knew the answer was to make sure that Zo had no excuse not to be successful. He was a young man who was resourceful; he had a big heart and he knew how to survive. He literally slept at my house and spent significant time with my family, including my children. So, I saw his potential to turn his life around in the right environment.

Zo stayed out there and he continued to play ball. I got to see him scrimmage, and he excelled inside and outside of the classroom. He ended up doing his two years and earned 48 credits. Of course, 48 credits is admirable when you're in school but in order to graduate, he needed to take 15 credit hours per semester. Instead of 15, he was taking 12 credit hours. He needed 60 hours to graduate from community college.

Zo's ultimate dream was to go to Division 1, but that was not an option with just 48 credits. We all knew Pound was about to come home. Concerned about the implications, Coach Sal said: "Yo, Cook, we've got to do something for Pound."

Coach Saul and the President of Laramie County Community College ended up getting Pound an extra year with a free scholarship because they loved him, and they knew if he went back home, he would have succumbed to the streets. To prevent this, they did something that was practically unheard of. Unlike most kids in America, Zo received a free year of school. He did his part, worked hard, and earned his associates degree.

He did not end up at a Division 1 school; he started attending a NAIA school called Langston University in Oklahoma City, an HBCU. He did his two years out there. He played ball. Now, he only has one or two classes left. He's still out there and he's holding it down. He doesn't want for anything. He's literally like Leonidas in the movie *300*. They just sent him out as a kid and he came back wearing a lion's coat. That's Pound. He was sent out into the wild and we knew that he was going to be alright because of his relationship with the adults who had poured into him. Even now, if we cannot reach him, we call his mother and then, he'll pick up the first ring for her.

In many ways, Pound is like another son to me. He's always welcome in my home. He'll say, "Cook, I need a place to stay the night." There is no question; he is a part of my extended family. Even my wife and kids love him. My oldest son adores him. I will even go so far as to say that I trust him with my life.

More Than Love

Perhaps as you were reading about Zo, you thought about movies like *Rudy, Remember the Titans,* or even *Antwone Fisher*? In each of these movies, a young man has lost his way and via the direction, mentorship, and most importantly, love of an adult leader, the young man learns the power of his own value.

Sounds magical and unbelievable, right? Well, the reality is that just like the adult role models in the aforementioned film examples, being a transformative leader means doing things that other people may deem as magical, unbelievable, and even radical. At the crux of most leaders' decision-making processes, is the question: Is this the best step to reach the desired outcomes?

Focusing on the love is more than rhetoric, and it is more than just emotions. It is about sacrifice. I knew that simply telling Zo to leave that lifestyle alone or to just stop hanging around certain people wasn't going to be enough. No matter how much he respected me or how much he knew right from wrong, that wasn't enough to counter a life that he had known and grown accustomed to. We had to think in non-linear terms; we had to think in extremes; we had to do what needed to be done, even if it went against conventional norms.

More than anything, we had to get Zo out of that environment. We needed him in a safe space where the pull of the streets would be dulled by the lure of a more promising future. By sending a young man, fully engrossed in Newark street life to Wyoming so that he could attend school in a more secluded and far less tempting environment, we created a different pathway for him.

With Zo's consent, he began a journey that radically changed his life. Not only did his outlook change, but so did his disposition. By taking him out of familiar surroundings, we helped him to expand his worldview and see the world through a different lens full of possibility and potentiality. Zo began to embrace his ability to positively contribute to society.

Like Zo, perhaps there is a member of your organization or team who needs transformative leadership. As a leader, are you equipped to see someone's needs even if it means making a radical adjustment? Are you prepared to sacrifice and go against the norm?

Is uprooting someone the answer for every student or team member that I encounter? No. Am I the first leader or educator to make a drastic decision to send someone away? No. In fact, many people send kids far away; however, they don't fly out on their own dime to make sure that someone else can stay in school or go shopping at Walmart to ensure that someone's basic needs are met. Although many may care, it is an act of true love to ensure that someone else doesn't want for anything. We even made sure that he had a summer job so that he could have additional money in his pocket. Furthermore, we helped fly him home during the holidays so that he could stay connected to his mom, nieces and nephews, and other family members.

We did this; and I share this, not for accolades or 'thank you' or any kind of recognition. All we wanted in return was for him to succeed. In fact, we are so committed to his life-long success, he has a gym teacher job waiting on him when he graduates.

Alfonzo's story illuminates how focusing on the love can help us to carve out solutions that require vision, innovation, and yes, even a little courage and radicalism. Had I only thought about Zo's education in traditional ways, I am not sure how his life would have turned out. What I do know is that this young man now has a chance to step into his own greatness and it all started by our willingness to focus on the love.

Chapter 9

THE FUTURE OF TRANSFORMATIVE LEADERSHIP

Henry Ford (2006) is credited with saying, "If I had asked people what they wanted, they would have said faster horses"(as cited in Watts, p. 154). As 21st century leaders, we may read this quote and chuckle, but the reality is that innovation and forward thinking have always been at the forefront of change. Simply operating a business, leading an industry, or even guiding students the same way that things have always been done is not an effective approach. As leaders, we not only have to think about solutions and problems, but we also have to consider what people need even if that need is not clearly known or expressed.

To reflect this, we have adopted, Promises Made, Promises Kept as our mantra:

> *Be the change you want to see. I Am The Change, I Am The Future, I was Born to Lead, I Am a Rough Rider!*

As a school leader, in particular, I knew that our traditional way of measuring success and student achievement was flawed. Most of the metrics are designed without students of color and poor students in mind. If the SAT is an indicator of success and a student does poorly on the exam, what does that say about that student's future? Similarly, if a state-administered exit exam is an earmark of success, what becomes of the student who fails? In other words, what do we do with those for whom traditional structures and systems do not work or have failed them? The answer is simple: We create new ones.

My industry is education; perhaps, your industry is business or entertainment or medicine. Regardless of your realm of influence, we have to create space for change, especially for those whom we lead. And it must go beyond just rhetoric, trendy hashtags, and YouTube videos. It must start with where we are and with the people who have entrusted us to lead them. For me, this all began with a desire to make sure that all of our students—not just those headed to college or the military—could see themselves as valued and treasured members of our community. We couldn't just do business as usual. We had to think outside of the box in order to get results.

Thinking outside of the box led to R.I.P. Upon first reading this, you may be thinking: *What does Rest In Peace have to do with leadership?* Actually, R.I.P. doesn't mean what you think it does. But just like most of my readers, I knew that it was an acronym that many of our students would already be familiar with. Rather than marinating an aura of negative centered around death, I thought what if I could take something and create something powerful that would help my babies truly understand the vast world out there just waiting for them to be great. From there, we came up with Relationships, Innovation, and Passion, R.I.P.

As the name suggests, this is not your typical organizational program. Being a boss in today's society means building relationships with others and for educational leaders, in particular, it means being attuned to our students' social and emotional learning. Specifically, at the School of Business and Finance, we now offer our students the ability to enroll in dual credit courses that allow them to graduate with an Associates Degree in Business Administration; they can earn 30 credit hours each their junior and senior years, and they can take classes on an actual college campus.

They can select one of the following pathways: Supply Chain Management, Entrepreneurship, Advance Manufacturing, or Accounting. To up the ante, students are given a stipend up to $2300 to ensure they can focus on studying and not earning money outside of school. Our Economic Opportunity Center focuses on four pathways: two- and four- year colleges and universities; trade schools; the armed forces; or direct career and life readiness.

As a leader, my goal is to remove barriers that prevent my staff from educating the students holistically, while building self-confidence and meaningful relationships from the moment scholars enter our doors until they are gainfully employed. For this to happen, I have to see passion as a derivative of love. When leaders do so, boundaries are penetrable and opportunities are unlimited.

As an outgrowth of R.I.P., we have crafted out ways for our students to discover, early on, who they are and what they aspire to do with their lives. I reached out to Damon Dash and we partnered to create a satellite of Dame Dash Studios on campus. We are building an innovative recording studio in our school which supersedes some professional recording studios in the industry. By leveraging my relationships with those outside of education, transformation becomes a reality.

The Passion to Wed Together Love with Vision

When I think about the future of education, I think about West Side High School. I imagine visitors coming into our school and envisioning our first floor as being similar to that of a mall. We already have a Capitol One branch that our students run. We have a laundry/cleaner, print shop, and boutique. We are building upon this and are adding a bodega, the studio, and soon, Poppington Clothing Line. We don't want our students to only learn just about selling merchandise, but we want them to embrace entrepreneurship, including designing, creating, branding, and marketing. We want them to be prepared for a future that requires them to be business savvy. It is a future that requires them, regardless of their backgrounds, to be capable of engaging with and supporting a global market and its demands.

R.I.P. is actually about breathing life into young people and helping them to see beyond today and their most immediate surroundings. By equipping them with tangible skills that they can take into their careers, college, or the military, we are empowering them to see their own greatness even before others can or will see it in them. Whether a student is interested in studio engineering and production or fashion design and merchandising, we recognize that if we can introduce them to industries that they can grow in and become passionate about, we will change not only their life trajectories but that of their families. That is the real power of transformational leadership—the ability to see beyond the right now—the ability to see what can happen and how it can happen if the right steps are put in place.

When leaders take the stance that they care deeply about the future of those whom they lead, they can begin to see beyond the deficits of right now. They can see beyond what they don't have to what they do have and how to best utilize their resources to reach their desired end goals. I bet that if you ask most leaders, they would tell you that they never have enough resources, tools, or people because most leaders dream big. However, that same group of leaders will also tell you that they don't focus on the shortcomings but rather possibility and probability. As simple as this may sound, it is the power of yet. Yet is a small and powerful word. It speaks of possibility, probability, and the likelihood of what's to come.

I remember watching *Sesame Street* with one of my sons a few years ago and Janelle Monae (2014) started singing about "The Power of Yet." Initially intrigued by the beat and the melodic tone, I shifted and started focusing on the lyrics. The song is a story about a group of characters, including Bert and Cookie Monster, who have dreams and goals. Bert wants to sing, but he can't hold a note. Cookie Monster wants to bake cookies, but every batch comes out burnt. In both instances, they could have quit after they failed. Yet, they kept trying and eventually, they became successful. As Monae sang and the two-minute clip concluded, I thought: Wow! What a message!

Yes, it was a simple children's song. Yet packed in there is a message that all transformational leaders can embrace. If we empower and equip people to believe in themselves, work steadfastly towards a goal, and commit to that goal, they will accomplish some degree of success. Their success will not be immediate and they may find that it will take more practice and skill; however, this does not mean that they are not purposed to do what they envision doing. As leaders focused on the love, we play an integral role in shaping the lives of others. Not only do we lead by example, but we help people see what potential they hold.

As Henry Ford suggested by the quote at the beginning of this chapter: We help people to understand what they need even before they know they need it. This may take the form of mentorship, advice, recommendations, a listening ear, or when required, redirecting destructive behavior. It is also important to note that transformation can also lead to resistance. Not everyone embraces change and not everyone will believe in people the way that you do and that's okay. Although we all have leadership potential, not everyone is called to be a leader and not everyone is called to be a transformational leader.

Yes, being a leader requires time, commitment, sacrifice, preparation, and skills. But being a transformational leader requires all of the aforementioned and even more. As you embark on your journey to be a transformational leader, I want to challenge you to: 1) Think about the untapped promise and potential of those who you lead; 2) Be fully present and remember that your team can only match your fly if you are leading by example; and 3) Most importantly, you must be willing to focus on the love.

In an ever changing society that pushes us towards only looking at the bottom line, and relying heavily on evidence and data, I suggest that when we *add love* to the leadership mix, our ability to influence, motivate and empower others will increase exponentially. Why? Because love is the key. Love is powerful. You can't underestimate the power of love.

APPENDIX

INSPIRATIONAL QUOTES ABOUT LOVE AND LEADERSHIP

(References are in the Works Consulted List)

Lance Secretan: "Leadership is not so much about technique and methods as it is about opening the heart. Leadership is about inspiration-of oneself and of others. Great leadership is about human experiences, not processes. Leadership is not a formula or a program, it is a human activity that comes from the heart and considers the heart of others. It is an attitude, not a routine."

Robert Greenleaf: "Good leaders must first become good servants."

Vince Lombardi: "Leaders aren't born, they are made. And they are made just like anything else, through hard work. And that's the price we'll have to pay to achieve that goal, or any goal."

Theodore Hesburgh: "The very essence of leadership is that you have to have a vision."

James Kouzes and Barry Posner: "There is nothing more

demoralizing than a leader who can't clearly articulate what we're doing."

John Kenneth Galbraith: "All of great leaders have had one characteristic in common; it was the willingness to confront unequivocally the major anxiety of their people in their time. This, and not much else, is the essence of leadership."

Peter Drucker: "The leaders who work most effectively, it seems to me, never say "I." And that's not because they have trained themselves not to say "I." They don't think "I." They think "we"; they think "team." They understand their job is to make the team function. They accept responsibility and don't sidestep it, but "we" gets the credit. This is what creates trust, and what enables you to get the task done."

Robert A Heinlein: "Love is that condition in which the happiness of another person is essential to your own."

Mónica C. Byrne-Jiménez and Irene H. Yoon: "Leaders must find other ways to lead. They should define the "habits of the heart" as harmony, courage, wisdom, and imagination. It is the combination of these habits that allow leadership with and through love."

Martin Luther King Jr.:
"He who is devoid of the power to forgive is devoid of the power to love."

"I have decided to stick with love. Hate is too great a burden to bear."

"Love is the only force capable of transforming an enemy into a friend."

"Darkness cannot drive out darkness: only light can do that. Hate cannot drive out hate; only love can do that."

"At the center of non-violence stands the principle of love."

"Man must evolve for all human conflict a method which rejects revenge, aggression and retaliation. The foundation of such a method is love."

WORKS CONSULTED

Alisic, E. (2012). Teachers' perspectives on providing support to children after trauma: a qualitative study. Sch. Psychol. Q. 27, 51–59. doi: 10.1037/a0028590

Alston, J. A. (2005). Tempered radicals and servant leaders: black females persevering in the superintendency. Edu. Administration Q. 41, 675–688. doi: 10.1177/0013161X04274275

Applebaum, E., Bailey, T., & Berg, P. (2000). Manufacturing Advantage: Why High Performance Work Systems Pay Off. Ithaca, NY: Cornell University Press.

Arnold, W. J. (1963). "Famous Firsts: High Priests of Efficiency." Business Week, June 22, 1963, pp. 100-104.

Baldoni, John (2008). How Trustworthy are you. Harvard Business Review. May 15, 2008 found on December 15, 2008 at https://hbr.org/2008/05/how-trustworthy-are-you

Baldwin, James (1961, 2020). NPR. Interview "To Be in a Rage, Almost All the Time." https://www.npr.org/2020/06/01/867153918/-to-be-in-a-rage-almost-all-thetime#:~:text=In%201961%2C%20author%20James%20Baldwin,time%20%E2%80%94%20and%20in%20one's%20work.

Bennis. Warren (2009). On Becoming a Leader. New York, NY: Basic Books.

Block, P., (2013). Stewardship: Choosing Service Over Self-Interest. San Francisco, CA: Jossey-Bass.

Boyatzis, R. E., & McKee, A. (2005). Resonant Leadership: Renewing Yourself and Connecting with Others through Mindfulness, Hope, and Compassion. Boston, MA: Harvard Business Review Press.

Boylan, M. (2008). The Good, the True, and the Beautiful: A Quest for Meaning. New York, NY: International Publishing Group.

Burns, J. M. (2010). Leadership. New York, NY: Harper.

Byrne-Jiménez MC and Yoon Irene (2019) Leadership as an Act of Love: Leading in Dangerous Times. Front. Educ. 3:117. doi: 10.3389/feduc.2018.00117

Caldwell, C., & Dixon, R. D. (2010). "Love, Forgiveness, and Trust: Critical Values of the Modern Leader." Journal of Business Ethics, Vol. 93, Iss. 1, pp. 91-101.

Caldwell, C., Atwijuka, S., & Okpala, C. O. (2018). "Compassionate Leadership in an Arms-Length World." Journal of Business and

Management.

Caldwell, C., Dixon, R. D., Floyd, L., Chaudoin, J., Post., J., & Cheokas, G. (2012). "Transformative Leadership: Achieving Unparalleled Excellence." Journal of Business Ethics, Vol 109, Iss. 2, pp. 175-187.

Caldwell, C., Hayes, L., & Long, D. (2010). "Leadership, Trustworthiness, and Ethical Stewardship." Journal of Business Ethics, Vol. 96, Iss. 4, pp. 497-512.

Campbell, Anita Effective Leadership Styles. American Express. May 18, 2016 found on October 30, 2020 at https://www.americanexpress.com/en-us/business/trends-and-insights/articles/effective-leadership-styles-business/

Capper, C. (2000). Life lessons and a loving epistemology: a response to Julie Liable's loving epistemology. Int. J. Qual. Stud. Edu. 13, 693–698. doi: 10.1080/09518390050211583

Conrad, D., and Kellar-Guenther, Y. (2006). Compassion fatigue, burnout, and compassion satisfaction among Colorado child protection workers. Child Abuse Neglect. 30, 1071–1080. doi: 10.1016/j.chiabu.2006.03.009

Covey, S. R. (1992). Principle-Centered Leadership. New York, NY: Simon & Schuster.

Dantley, M. E. (2003). Critical spirituality: enhancing transformative leadership through critical theory and African American prophetic spirituality. Int. J. Leadership Edu. 6, 3–17. doi: 10.1080/136031202200006998

Dantley, M. E. (2005). African American spirituality and Cornel West's notions of prophetic pragmatism: restructuring educational leadership in American urban schools. Edu. Administration Q. 41, 651–674. doi: 10.1177/0013161x04274274

Dantley, M. E. (2010). Successful leadership in urban schools: principals and critical spirituality, a new approach to reform. J. Negro Edu. 79, 214–219. Available online at: http://www.jstor.org/stable/20798344

Dantley, M. E., and Tillman, L. C. (2010). "Social justice and moral transformative leadership," in Leadership for Social Justice: Making Revolutions in Education, ed C. Marshall and M. Oliva (Boston, MA: Allyn & Bacon Publishers), 19–34.

Darder, A. (1998). Teaching as an Act of Love: Reflections on Paulo Freire and His Contributions to Our Lives and Work. San Bernadino, CA: California Association for Bilingual Education.

DePree, M. (2004). Leadership is an Art. New York, NY: Crown.

Doniach, N., & Kahane, A. (Eds). (1996). The Oxford English-Hebrew Dictionary. Oxford, UK: Oxford University Press.

Drucker, Peter (2006). The Effective Executive. New York, NY: Harper Collins Press.

Duncan-Andrade, J. M. R., and Morrell, E. (2008). The Art of Critical Pedagogy: Possibilities for Moving from Theory to Practice in Urban Schools. New York, NY: Peter Lang. doi: 10.3726/b12771

Durlak, J. A., Weissberg, R. P., Dymnicki, A. B., Taylor, R. D., and Schellinger, K. B. (2011). The impact of enhancing students' social and emotional learning: a meta-analysis of school-based universal interventions. Child Dev. 82, 405–432. doi: 10.1111/j.1467-8624.2010.01564.x

E., Bailey, T., & Berg, P. (2000). Manufacturing Advantage: Why High Performance Work Systems Pay Off. Ithaca, NY: Cornell University Press.

Eisenhower, Dwight (2013). As cited in Ty Kisel Forbes. February 5. 2013 found September 15, 2020 at thttps://www.forbes.com/sites/tykiisel/2013/02/05/without-it-no-real-success-is-possible/?sh=35b1b400e491

Elmore, R. F., and Burney, D. (1997). Investing in Teacher Learning:

Staff Development and Instructional Improvement: Community School District 2, New York City. New York, NY: National Commission on Teaching and America's Future and the Consortium for Policy Research in Education.

Ford, Henry (2006). As cited in Steven Watts. Henry Ford: The People's Tycoon. New York, NY: Vintage Books.

Freire, P. (1970). Pedagogy of the Oppressed. New York, NY: Bloomsbury Publishing.

Freire, P. (1998). Teachers as Cultural Workers: Letters to Those Who Dare Teach. Boulder, CO: Westview.

Friedman, M. (1970). "The Social Responsibility of Business Is to Increase Its Profits." New York Times Magazine, September 13, 1970.

Fromm, E. (2000). The Art of Loving: The Centennial Edition. New York, NY: Continuum Publishers.

Galbraith, John Kenneth (2017). As cited in Smart Brief. July 17, 2017 and found online September 1, 2020 at https://www.smartbrief.com/branded/3E572E11-3FBC-11D5-AD13-000244141872/DDD64665-5401-448E-8E43-3CEBCB1C5D1D

Grant, Adam (2013). Give and Take: Why Helping Others Drives Our Success. New York, NY: Penguin Press.

Greenleaf, R. K. (2015). The Servant as Leader. Atlanta, GA: Greenleaf Center for Servant Leadership.

Gulbrandsen, K., & Caldwell, C. (In Press). "Love and Humility – Enhancing Leadership Success" in Love: The Heart of Leadership. Caldwell, C., & Anderson, V. (Eds.). Hauppage, NY: NOBA Publishers.

Halpern, R. (1999). After-school Programs for Low-Income Children: Promises and Challenges. Future Child. Fall 9 (2), 81-95.

Heinlan, Robert (2013). As cited in Philosiblog. August 19, 2003 found on December 1, 2020 at https://philosiblog.com/2013/08/19/love-is-that-condition-in-which-the-happiness-of-another-person-is-essential-to-your-own/

Hesburgh, Theodore (2015). As cited in Jared Dees Medium. November 1, 2020 at https://medium.com/@jareddees/the-very-essence-of-leadership-is-that-you-have-to-have-a-vision-it-s-got-to-be-a-vision-you-3fa0fa9f355d

Hernandez, M. (2012). "Toward an Understanding of the Psychology of Stewardship." Academy of Management Review, Vol. 37, Iss. 2, pp.

172-193 and Caldwell, C., Hayes, L.,& Long, D. (2010). "Leadership, Trustworthiness, and Ethical Stewardship." Journal of Business Ethics, Vol. 96, Iss. 4, pp. 497-512

hooks, bell. (1994). Teaching to Transgress: Education as the Practice of Freedom. New York, NY: Routledge.

hooks, bell. (2001). All About Love: New Visions. New York, NY: Harper Perennial.

hooks, bell. (2009). Belonging: A Culture of Place. New York, NY: Routledge.

Jobs, Steve (2018). As cited in Carmine Gallo. Steve Jobs Followed 7 Unbreakable Laws. Inc. August 7, 2018 and found online October 20, 2020. https://www.inc.com/carmine-gallo/steve-jobs-followed-7-unbreakable-laws-of-success-that-apply-to-any-business.html

Johnson, L. (2014). Culturally responsive leadership for community empowerment. Multicult. Educ. Rev. 6, 145–170.

Kay, K., and Greenhill, V. (2013). The Leader's Guide to 21st Century Education: 7 Steps for Schools and Districts. Boston, MA: Pearson Education.

Keating, A. L. (2013). Transformation Now! Toward a Post-

Oppositional Politics of Change. Urbana: University of Illinois Press.

Kessler, R. (2000). The Soul of Education: Helping Students Find Connection, Compassion, and Character at School. Alexandria, VA: ASCD.

Khalifa, M. (2018). Culturally Responsive School Leadership. Cambridge, MA: Harvard Education Press.

King, M. L. Jr. (1967). Beyond Vietnam: A Time to Break Silence. Speech delivered at Riverside Church, New York, NY. Available online at: https://kinginstitute.stanford.edu/king-papers/documents/beyond-vietnam

King, Martin Luther, Jr. (1963, 2010). Strength to Love. Minneapolis, MN: Fortress Press.

Kouzes, J. M., & Posner, B. Z. (2017). The Leadership Challenge: How to Get Extraordinary Things Done in Organizations(6thed.). San Francisco, CA: Jossey-Bass.

Lewin, K., Lippitt, R., & White, R. K. (1999/1939). Patterns of aggressive behavior in experimentally created "social climates". In M. Gold (Ed.), *The complete social scientist: a Kurt Lewin reader* (pp. 227–250). Washington, DC: American Psychological Association.

Liable, J. C. (2000). A loving epistemology: what I hold critical in my life, faith, and profession. Int. J. Qual. Stud. Edu. 13, 683–692. doi: 10.1080/09518390050211574

Lippman, Walter (2019). As cited in Bruce Tulgan. Stick to the Basics: The Leadership Wisdom of Dave. Christiansen. July 18, 2019 found on December 18, 2020 at https://www.linkedin.com/pulse/stick-basics-leadership-wisdom-dave-christiansen-bruce-tulgan/

Lombardi, Vince (2020). As cited in Matthew Newell. What You Can Learn From Vince Lombardi's Timeless Leadership Wisdom. November 2, 2020 found November 15, 2020 at https://inc.com/partners-in-Leadership-what-you-can-learn-from-lomardis-timeless-leadership-wisdom.html

Mann & Harter (2016). "The Worldwide Employee Engagement Crisis." Gallup Workplace, January 7, 2016 and found online on March 9, 2019 at ttps://www.gallup.com/workplace/236495 h/worldwide-employee-engagement-crisis.aspx.

Merriam-Webster Dictionary (2020). November 30, 2020 and found December 3, 2020 https://www.merriam-webster.com/

Meyerson, D. E., and Scully, M. A. (1995). Crossroads tempered radicalism and the politics of ambivalence and change. Organ. Sci. 6, 585–600.

Monae, Janelle. (2014). The Power of Yet. Sesame Street. September 10, 2014 and found online October 1, 2020 at https://www.youtube.com/watch?v=XLeUvZvuvAs.

Moseley, Corey (2020). 7 Reasons Why Collaboration is Key. September 14, 2020 found December 15, 2020 at https://blog.jostle.me/blog/why-collaboration-is-important

Myers, Dwight. (1989). I Got Nothing But Love for You. Big Tyme. July 1, 2020 and found online November 31, 2020 at https://en.wikipedia.org/wiki/Big_Tyme

Murtadha-Watts, K. (1999). "Spirited sisters: spirituality and the activism of African American women in educational leadership," in School Leadership: Expanding the Horizons of the Mind and Spirit: 7th Yearbook of the National Council of Professors of Educational Administration, ed L. T. Fenwick (Lancaster, PA: Technomic Publishing Company), 155–167.

Nee-Benham, A., Maenette, K. P., and Cooper, J. E. (1998). Let My Spirit Soar! Narratives of Diverse Women in School Leadership. Thousand Oaks, CA: Corwin Press.

Nhat Hanh, T. (2015). How to Love. Berkeley, CA: Parallax Press.

Overvold, G. E. (1987). The imperative of organizational harmony: a critique of contemporary human relations theory. J. Business Ethics 6, 559–565. doi: 10.1007/BF00383747

Oxford University Press (2010). Oxford Essential Arabic Dictionary. Oxford, UK: Oxford University Press.

Oxford University Press, (2008). The Oxford New Greek Dictionary: The Essential Resource Revised and Updated. Oxford, UK: Oxford University Press.

Palmer, P. J. (1983). To Know as We are Known: Education as a Spiritual Journey. New York, NY: HarperCollins Publishers.

Pava, M. (2003). Leading with Meaning: Using Covenantal Leadership to Build a Better Organization. New York, NY: St. Martin's Press.

Peck, M. S. (2003). The Road Less Traveled, 25thAnniversary Edition: A New Psychology of Love, Traditional Values, and Spiritual Growth. New York:, NY Simon & Schuster.

Pfeffer, J. (1998). The Human Equation: Building Profits by Putting People First. Boston, MA: Harvard Business School Press.

Poplin, M. (1992). The leader's new role: looking to the growth of teachers. Edu. Leadership 49, 10–11.

Ross, W.D. (2014). The Complete Works of Aristotle. New York, NY: Holy Books.

Sarnoff, David (1986). As cited in Kenneth Bilby. The General: David Sarnoff and the Rise of the Communications Industry. New York, NY: HarperCollins Publishers.

Sahrish Ahmad, Elizabeth R. Peterson, Karen E. Waldie and Susan M. B. Morton.

Scheurich, J. J. (1998). Highly successful and loving, public elementary schools populated mainly by low-SES children of color: core beliefs and cultural characteristics. Urban Edu. 33, 451–491. doi: 10.1177/0042085998033004001

Secretan, Lance (2010). The Spark, the Flame, and the Torch. Copper Mountain, CO: The Secretan Center, Inc.

Shakespeare, William. Julius Ceasar. Folger Library. New York, NY: Washington Square Press, 1992.

Shields, C. M. (2004). Dialogic leadership for social justice: overcoming pathologies of silence. Edu. Administration Q. 40, 109–132. doi: 10.1177/0013161X03258963

Solomon, R. C. (1993). Ethics and Excellence: Cooperation and Integrity in Business. Oxford, UK: Oxford University Press.

Stanmyre, Matthew (2020). This rockstar principal made a name on Ellen and Oprah. But it all started with basketball. Feburary 16, 2020 found December 17, 2020 at https://www-nj-com.cdn.ampproject.org c/s/www.nj.com/highschoolsports/2020/02/this-rockstar-principal-made-a-name-on-ellen-ane-oprah-but-it-all-started -with basketball.html?outputType=amp

Steward, Glenn (2017). Developing Super Leaders. April 29, 2017 found November 30, 2020 at https://developingsuperleaders.wordpress.com/2017/04/29/if-your-leadership-is-truly-grounded-in-love-youll-always-land-in-the-category-of-a-good-leader-glenn-c- stewart/#:~:text= com%20site %20ever- ,%E2%80%9CIf%20your%20LEADERSHIP%20is %20truly%20groun ded%20in%20LOVE%2C%20you',Stewart)

Theoharis, G. (2007). Social justice educational leaders and resistance: toward a theory of social justice leadership. Edu. Administration Q. 43, 221–258. doi: 10.1177/0013161X06293717

White, M. D. (2010)."Loving Yourself: How Important Is It?" Psychology Today, April 29, 2010 found on January 21, 2019 at https://www.psychologytoday.com/us/blog/maybe-its-just-me/201004/loving-yourself-how-important-is-it

Wren, D. A. (2004). The History of Management Thought. Hoboken, NJ: Wiley.

Zavada, J. (2018). "What is Agape Love in the Bible?" ThoughtCo. July 31, 2018 found on January 21, 2019 at https://www.thoughtco.com/agape-love-in-the-bible-700675

ABOUT THE AUTHOR

Akbar H. Cook Sr. was born and raised in Newark's West Ward. He attended Essex Catholic High School, where he excelled as a student and basketball player. Mr. Cook attended St. Catherine's College in Kentucky on two basketball scholarships before graduating with a Bachelor of Arts degree in Education from Florida Atlantic University, a Division 1 University in Boca Raton, Florida. He went on to receive a Master's Degree in Administration and Supervision from St. Peter's University in Jersey City in 2006.

Mr. Cook's love for children and basketball led him to Newark Vocational School in 2008, where he became head coach of the boys' basketball team. From the head basketball coach position, he was promoted to Vice Principal in 2012. In 2014, he was assigned to West Side High School as the Vice Principal. Mr. Cook is well known for having a stern, yet caring presence in the lives of many of Newark's youth. His desire to uplift and educate children is always at the forefront of his work in Newark Public Schools. Mr. Cook's passion to improve his community and impact children's lives has led him to volunteer in food kitchens and participate in Christmas tree and toy drives. He also organizes recreational activities for Newark Public School students and works closely with the Newark Police Department to ensure safe transportation for all students after school functions. In the summer of 2016, Mr. Cook started the Lights On Program at West Side High School from the peak hours of 6-11 p.m., to ensure that our students and other young adults in the community are safe during peak crime hours. His vision for Lights On became a reality after he lost students to gun violence.

Mr. Akbar Cook was named the Principal of West Side High School for the 2018-2019 school year! One month into his new role as Principal, Mr. Cook had his grand opening for a laundromat at West Side High School which was his project to help ameliorate bullying concerns for students who were displaced and had no funds or access to washing machines. The bullying resulted in excessive school absences and after the laundromat installation, the attendance rates increased significantly. The initiative has been named "Washing Bullying Away".

After being featured on *The Star-Ledger*, and the success of the newly installed laundromat reached the producers of *The Ellen DeGeneres Show* who invited Principal Cook as a guest of the show on two separate occasions where he secured over $100,000 from DeGeneres and a year's supply of food from General Mills for the food pantry. His Lights On segment on *CBS Evening News* garnered the attention of Oprah Winfrey who visited the school and dropped off a generous donation of $500,000 to ensure the longevity of the Lights On Program. He continues to create new initiatives such as the development of the Urban Farm on campus, a built-in soccer pitch, and a brand-new kitchen for Home Economics. Principal Cook is a divine leader who builds other leaders just like himself while focusing on the love.

In addition to serving as Principal of West Side High School, he also serves as program director of Great Newark LifeCamp; a summer camp for inner city youth. Akbar Cook resides in NJ with his wife and three sons.

To book Akbar Cook for workshops, consulting or speaking engagements, please visit us at:

CookEducationalSolutions.com

PrincipalCook23@gmail.com

Made in the USA
Middletown, DE
30 October 2023

41661419R00066